Digital Textuality

DIGITAL TEXTUALITY

PAOLA TRIMARCO

© Paola Trimarco 2015

All rights reserved. No reproduction, copy or transmission of this publication may be made without written permission.

No portion of this publication may be reproduced, copied or transmitted save with written permission or in accordance with the provisions of the Copyright, Designs and Patents Act 1988, or under the terms of any licence permitting limited copying issued by the Copyright Licensing Agency, Saffron House, 6–10 Kirby Street, London EC1N 8TS.

Any person who does any unauthorized act in relation to this publication may be liable to criminal prosecution and civil claims for damages.

The author has asserted her right to be identified as the author of this work in accordance with the Copyright, Designs and Patents Act 1988.

First published 2015 by
PALGRAVE

Palgrave in the UK is an imprint of Macmillan Publishers Limited, registered in England, company number 785998, of 4 Crinan Street, London N1 9XW.

Palgrave Macmillan in the US is a division of St Martin's Press LLC, 175 Fifth Avenue, New York, NY 10010.

Palgrave is a global imprint of the above companies and is represented throughout the world.

Palgrave® and Macmillan® are registered trademarks in the United States, the United Kingdom, Europe and other countries.

ISBN 978–1–137–33496–1

This book is printed on paper suitable for recycling and made from fully managed and sustained forest sources. Logging, pulping and manufacturing processes are expected to conform to the environmental regulations of the country of origin.

A catalogue record for this book is available from the British Library.

A catalog record for this book is available from the Library of Congress.

Typeset by MPS Limited, Chennai, India.

Printed and bound by CPI Group (UK) Ltd, Croydon, CR0 4YY

Contents

List of Figures and Tables viii

Acknowledgements ix

List of Abbreviations x

1	**Introduction to Digital Textuality**	1
	Introduction	1
	What is digital textuality?	1
	Digital talk	3
	Digital texts	7
	Digital literacy	9
	Overview of critical approaches to digital textuality	12
	Conclusions	16
	Sample project	16
	Further reading	17
2	**Learning and Digital Textuality**	18
	Introduction	18
	Digital literacy and education	19
	Learning environments	21
	Students' online discussions	24
	Wikipedia	29
	Conclusions	33
	Sample project	34
	Further reading	34
3	**Social Networking Sites**	36
	Introduction	36
	What are SNSs?	37

SNSs and discourse communities 40
Presentation of the self 42
SNS: digital texts 46
SNS: digital talk 51
Conclusions 53
Sample projects 54
Further reading 54

4 Digital News 56
Introduction 56
Mainstream media 59
News blogs 61
Ideational meaning in digital news 65
Interpersonal meaning in digital news 67
Textual meaning in digital news 71
Conclusions 73
Sample projects 74
Further reading 74

5 Digital Poetry 76
Introduction 76
Analysing multimodal texts 77
Text montage poetry 81
Hyperpoetry 84
Animated poetry 88
Conclusions 93
Sample project 94
Further reading 95

6 Fiction and Collaboration Online 97
Introduction 97
Text World Theory 99
Flight Paths 102
Ficly 111
Conclusions 117
Sample projects 117
Further reading 118

7	**Hypertext Fiction**	**120**
	Introduction	120
	What is hypertext fiction?	120
	Interpersonal meaning and reader empowerment	122
	Textual meaning in hypertext fiction	124
	Patchwork Girl	126
	Twelve Blue	130
	'Samantha in Winter'	135
	Conclusions	137
	Sample projects	138
	Further reading	139
8	**Genre Hybrids and Superdiversity**	**141**
	Introduction	141
	Genres	142
	Genre hybrids	145
	Urban Dictionary	148
	Digital essays	150
	Superdiversity	153
	The Buddha Smiled	155
	Conclusions	157
	Sample projects	159
	Further reading	159
Glossary		161
Bibliography		166
Index		173

List of Figures and Tables

Figures

1.1	Examples of emoji	4
5.1	Screen image from 'How my brain betrays me'	78
5.2	'The Shadow' by Stef Zelynskyj	82
5.3	Second screen image from 'Sydney's Siberia'	85
5.4	Screen image from 'Sydney's Siberia'	86
5.5	Screen image from 'How my brain betrays me'	92
6.1	Summary of Text World Theory	102
6.2	Screen image from Chapter 1 of *Flight Paths*	106
6.3	Screen image from Chapter 3 of *Flight Paths*	107
6.4	Screen image from Chapter 6 of *Flight Paths*	109
7.1	Title page of *Patchwork Girl*	123
7.2	Screen image from *Patchwork Girl*	128
7.3	Screen image from *Patchwork Girl* showing story map	129

Tables

3.1	Summary of a tag search	49
4.1	Hyperlinks in mainstream media sites	72
4.2	Hyperlinks in news blogs	72
6.1	Summary of world-building elements in Chapters 1 and 3 of *Flight Paths*	105
7.1	Lexical cohesion across three lexia in *Twelve Blue*	134
8.1	Hybridity examples from a digital essay	152

Acknowledgements

The author and publisher wish to thank the following for permission to reproduce copyright material:

Siddarth Singh for extracts from The Buddha Smiled, in Chapters 1 and 8. *The Guardian*, *The Independent* and *The Daily Telegraph* for extracts in Chapter 4. Kate Barton and Miriam Barr for the images in Figures 5.1 and 5.5 and for the reproduction of their text 'How my brain betrays me' in Chapter 5. Stef Zelynskyj for the image in Figure 5.2. Jason Nelson for images in Figures 5.3 and 5.4 and for extracts from 'Sydney's Siberia'. James Andrews for the reproduction of the text 'Seattle Drift' in Chapter 5. Kevin Lawver for postings to Ficly.com appearing in Chapter 6. Kate Pullinger and Chris Joseph for images in Figures 6.2, 6.3 and 6.4 and for extracts from *Flight Paths* in Chapter 6. *London Evening Standard* for the news report in Chapter 6 (linked to the *Flight Paths* website). Eastgate Systems for images in Figures 7.1, 7.2 and 7.3, and for extracts from *Patchwork Girl* by Shelley Jackson and *Twelve Blue* by Michael Joyce in Chapter 7. Paul Stephens for an extract from 'Samantha in Winter' in Chapter 7. *Times Higher Education* for a tweet by Paul Jump in Chapter 8.

The author is indebted to the students of a Digital Textuality course at University Campus Suffolk, UK, who engaged with many of the examples in this volume, and in particular, those students who provided examples of their own digital texts (Francesca Mae Randall, Gemma Jamieson and Tom Ratcliffe) and students who read draft chapters (Aly Dobson, Nichola Carton and Cara Moran). Gratitude is also expressed to others who read and commented on chapters: David Owen, Nadia Marzocco, Kate Lawrence and Sara Whiteley, as well as to colleagues and associates who granted permission to use their tweets: Nigel Ball, Ian Baxter and Uday Nair. And finally, this book would not be possible without the guidance, support and sense of humour provided by Paul Stevens and Aléta Bezuidenhout.

List of Abbreviations

CA	Conversational Analysis
CDA	Critical Discourse Analysis
CMC	Computer Mediated Communication
DA	Discourse Analysis
IRC	Internet Relay Chat
NLS	New Literacy Studies
SFL	Systemic Functional Linguistics
SNS	Social Network Site
TWT	Text World Theory
VLE	virtual learning environments

1 Introduction to Digital Textuality

Introduction

According to Internet World Stats, by 2012 over 2.4 billion people were using the internet. It is no surprise that linguists have turned to the internet to study language in use. The ways in which language is used in new media technologies is central to this book, along with the linguistic approaches applied to the analysis of these texts.

In this first chapter we will begin by defining what is meant by digital textuality. From there the distinction is made between 'digital talk' and 'digital text' for the purposes of linguistic analysis, though both are studied in this book as forms of digital textuality. We will then consider how interacting with digital texts, referred to as digital literacy, can be approached in broad terms set out by New Literacy Studies (NLS) as types of **literacy practices**, studied with respect to social contexts. We conclude with an overview of critical approaches which have been used to describe and analyse digital texts. Upon completion of this chapter, you will be able to use key terms when linguistically describing digital texts and have a basic understanding of critical approaches in order to continue to explore digital texts in the following chapters.

What is digital textuality?

In simple terms, digital texts are those texts which are produced to be read in digital formats, namely computers. While all word-processed texts are produced digitally and can be read on computer screens, this particular format is just the starting point for digital texts. Developments in mobile phones and tablets are also used in the production and reception of digital texts. We use the term 'digital textuality' to take into account the way we use digital texts and the contexts within which we use them.

As we are studying texts produced with digital technologies, a key concept is the idea that digital texts are different from traditionally printed texts. We can express this difference by considering the way digital texts use the 'affordances' of technology which are not available to users of printed forms. The term *affordance* was first used in 1977 by psychologist James L. Gibson to describe the 'action possibilities' brought on by a particular environment. This term has since evolved for use in analysing digital media to refer to both the possibilities and constraints for action in various digital spaces. Barton and Lee (2013) make the following salient points about the affordances of digital texts: 'The internet is not limitless and that is why looking at affordances is essential'; and 'It is the ways in which people can act within the affordances of designed spaces that create different possibilities for writing' (p. 29).

One of the chief affordances of digital communication has been the use of **multimodality**. Given the easy access to images, video clips and podcasts, digital texts are frequently multimodal, where for example images and sound can accompany written texts. For this reason analysing digital textuality involves the analysis of linguistic, visual and auditory elements, though we are restricted by the affordances of this printed book to the analysis of words and images. In upcoming chapters, we will employ the closely related fields of social semiotic and multimodal stylistic approaches to language study as they include frameworks for analysing images.

At various points in this book the analyses used will consider features of context and the concept of identity as both impact upon and create meaning and communication styles. External contexts are vast and often difficult to take into account. In online communication, as in all interaction, context includes social and cultural understandings and practices. But such contexts are not always made accessible to linguists analysing the texts or discourses which are embedded in these contexts. The anonymity of participants in online environments also poses challenges when considering the presence and performance of identity, and the ways in which participants in online communication express identity have been much written about since the early days of the internet. Initially, theorists worked from the premise that most online identity was a 'mask' which was different from 'real life' (Turkle, 1997). More recently, theorists have recognised that offline and online identity construction are not necessarily separate but can in fact overlap (Thurlow et al., 2004). Warschauer's (2004) summary of current perspectives on identity is also useful here by noting that 'identity in the postmodern era has been found to be multiple, dynamic and conflictual, based not on a permanent sense of self, but rather on the choices that individuals make in different circumstances over time' (p. 94). While recognition of multiple and dynamic identities are characteristic of face-to-face interaction, online environments can arguably allow more opportunities for developing identities. This is particularly marked in social media, where for example Facebook is all about presenting one's identity to the world; we will return to identity as part of linguistic analysis in Chapter 3.

Digital talk

Digital talk broadly refers to the texts found in Computer Mediated Communication (CMC), which, as its name suggests, involves using computers to communicate in ways similar to conversation. Early studies of CMC focused on organisational uses of computers with an interest in group decision-making in work environments. The direction of CMC scholarship has dramatically changed over the years, as now the social uses of CMC are at the forefront of research. For linguists, such research can be divided into two categories: approaches along the lines of discourse analysis and those approaches which look to the specific language used in these contexts.

In order to consider these approaches, we need to start with the fundamental notion that, unlike conversation, digital talk is written. It can be either synchronous, as in live chat rooms, or asynchronous, as in most discussion forums, e-mails and blogs. Synchronous communication is closer to oral conversation, in terms of participants being present in the online space at the same time though they are in different geographical environments; in these ways, synchronous communication is similar to phone conversations. Asynchronous communication is characterised by participants not necessarily being online at the same time, with the time lapses between contributions to a conversation ranging from minutes to months. Both synchronous and asynchronous communication share similarities with oral conversation, such as informal **registers**, turn-taking and the general dynamics of 'talk'.

Whether synchronous or asynchronous, CMC involves written communication (with notable exceptions, such as Skype video conferencing) which has evolved using the technical affordances of digital communication to produce texts of words and symbols. Many of these symbols have arisen from the creative use of punctuation, such as emoticons ;) and :(, for example, but we also have built into many online environments other picture symbols used to communicate. For example, the growing use of emoji, such as those in Figure 1.1, contributes meaning to digital talk. Emoji originated in Japan in text messages and come from '*e*', meaning 'picture' and '*moji*' meaning 'character'. Incidentally, the three emoji in Figure 1.1 represent 'alien', 'smiling imp' and 'cake'.

Another example of the affordances of online environments creating a style of communication can be seen in the tendencies in Internet Relay Chat (IRC) to produce third-person present tense descriptions, such as 'Chris is in a bad mood' and 'Lynn waves', to describe the

Figure 1.1 Examples of emoji
Source: Unicode fonts

writer's state of mind (Herring, 2013, p. 11). These examples have a 'performative flavour' which might be seen as working within the constraints of interacting without physically seeing other participants; it could also be seen as an easier and quicker way of expressing a tone of voice than writing phrases and sentences. Other interesting tendencies of IRCs can be found in the use of just a name of another participant as well as what have been called 'null-emotes'; these are turns which are intentionally left blank so that only the username appears. Such utterances can be loaded with pragmatic ambiguity, and therefore hold different meanings in the contexts of different online conversations.

In this example from an internet chat room (Second Life), we can see extensive use of emoticons and punctuation to create meaning not only through emotion, but also in making images – even that of a cow (user names have been anonymised):

1. [08:29] AA: I ♥ THIS SONG !!!
2. [08:29] R: ♪♪♪♪♫♫♪ APPPPPPLLLLAAAUUUSSSSEEEEEEE♪♪♪♪♫♫♪
3. [08:29] HR: wasn't sure if that was your thumb she's under or not, Crash
4. [08:29] KD: ♥«¨´°•KEEP LIVE MUSIC ALIVE.°•´¨»♥
5. [08:29] KD: +*'*•.¸AND IF POSSIBLE THIS VENUE+*'*•.¸
6. [08:29] KD: ♥«¨´°•THANK YOU!!!.°•´¨»♥
7. [08:29] KD: (*•.¸♥¸.•*´)TIP THIS GREAT MUSICIAN(*•.¸♥¸.•*´)
8. [08:29] FT: !!! A*P*P*L*A*U*S*E !!!
9. [08:30] KD: *.¸¸.•*´*•TP YOUR FRIENDS TO COME PARTY WITH US*.¸¸.•*´*•
10. [08:31] KD: ** Tipping…it's not just for cows! **
11. [08:31] KD: ^___^
12. [08:31] KD: \ (oo) _____
13. [08:31] KD: (___) \   )V \
14. [08:31] KD: ||----w |
15. [08:31] KD: || ||
16. [08:31] KD: PERFORMERS & VENUES
17. [08:31] KD: LOVE TO GET TIPPED TOO!

(*Source*: https://my.secondlife.com/cherin.cluny/snapshots/4f5735296fd4a91d12000001)

This example illustrates how online chat can be similar to oral conversation, as it is in an informal **register**, has contributions that resemble turns and the participants in this segment are for the most part on the same topic about music and pretending that they are having an online party, as if in a virtual space. We can also see adjacency pairs in the response in line 8, where the user applauds the imaginary musician. However, an example of where this interaction differs from face-to-face conversation occurs in line 3, where the participant does not seem to be responding to any nearby posting. In fact, a fuller account of this interaction appears to go on for some 100 lines of turns; judging by the contributions of KD, several threads of conversational topics seem to be occurring simultaneously. For analysts, it is hard to tell where threads begin and end as there are interruptions between related turns.

The other way in which this segment of IRC is unlike oral conversation is in the fact that users are aware that their texts are being read, and use this affordance of the chat room to great effect. The clever use of punctuation keys and the separate lines for each turn have allowed KD to create the image of a cow (lines 11–15).

IRC is an example of synchronous communication. Digital talk which is asynchronous can be found in 'comment' postings and discussion forums. Like the example of IRC above, these asynchronous communications are more talk than text as they are based on turn-taking. However, without the immediacy of synchronous interaction, examples such as emails could act as stand-alone texts and these might be more digital text than digital talk. As we will see in Chapter 3, where we examine social media, asynchronous communication can also branch out into networks of conversations and can involve many passive participants who read postings but do not produce any themselves (commonly known as 'lurkers').

As we have seen above, a key feature of communicating with digital talk is the way in which participants draw from semiotic resources, such as punctuation, emoticons and emoji. It is also worth considering the linguistic resources or the type of language employed in these environments. The idea of 'netspeak', 'e-chat' and a 'language variety' to describe CMC was part of the first wave of linguistic analyses of the internet. For Crystal (2001) there were also categories of internet language, for example, the language of chat rooms and the language of emails. But these ideas have been challenged. For example, given the range of uses and contextual settings of emails, the idea of them having common linguistic features is easily diluted. These views, as well as other studies, suggest that it would be more accurate to examine CMC not so much by **genre** (such as e-mail, discussion forum etc.) as in terms of communities.

For many researchers the idea of studying communities seems especially apt for online communication as it captures a sense of interpersonal connection among participants as well as the shared interests and online contexts. One way of developing this is to consider communities of practice, which considers groups of people working together with a common goal who develop shared ways of interacting (Wenger, 1998). A similar approach to online communities comes from the notion of a discourse community, first introduced by Swales (1990) to describe a group which shares common goals and purposes and communicates these via mutually understood genres and registers. Whereas communities of practice as a concept focuses more on the activities and practices, discourse communities focus more on the distinctions between speech communities. Current scholarship reflects this sense of CMC having features of the language of particular groups or communities of users in particular contexts, as opposed to early research focusing on the computer environment as the main source of language features. This, however, is not to say that those participating online see themselves as part of a community, but here the notion of community is useful for the perspective of analysing the language of online communication.

> **Activity**
>
> Go to a public chat room, such as those available on Second Life and Yahoo, and make a screen shot of a stretch of digital talk. Identify features of conversation for this stretch of digital talk, considering ways in which tone of voice is produced in the written medium.

Digital texts

As we will see throughout this book, digital texts come in many forms and genres and are as diverse as texts in traditionally printed formats.

Examples of digital texts, as opposed to digital talk, can be found in news sites, e-zines, personal and company websites and any website which contains fictional and non-fictional stories. Even though these examples are for the most part digital texts, elements of digital talk often co-exist at the same websites in the form of comment postings and discussion forums, along with links to social media, such as Facebook and Twitter.

Below is a digital text, taken from a blog called 'The Buddha Smiled', which is more digital text than digital talk; in other words, it can be solely read, without the reader participating as in a conversation:

Wednesday, February 27, 2013

Sexism, Sexuality and that Damn Oscars Song

Seth MacFarlane's hosting of this year's Academy Awards ceremony is, by now, a well-critiqued car crash. The articles here, here and here are well-argued, analytical and clearly document why the racism and sexism his jokes were based on is deplorable.

But one aspect of his routine that might have been overlooked is the chorus that supported MacFarlane during his opening number, We Saw Your Boobs. MacFarlane, a trained singer and pianist, was backed in that crass and tasteless number by the Gay Men's Chorus of Los Angeles (GMCLA), an organisation that, according to its website, has the vision to sing 'for a future free from homophobia and all other discrimination'.

Unlike digital talk, the text has a heading, is broken into paragraphs and has more full sentences in it. In contrast to the informality we saw in the IRC example, this is written in a semi-formal register and has hyperlinked text (which appears as underlined). This text clearly uses the affordances of internet technology in the way it uses hyperlinks to articles in the second line, using the deictic adverb '*here*'; this occurrence of **deixis** is also somewhat informal and more characteristic of speech than text writing. The hyperlinks themselves extend this text with more information and support for the ideas presented. What also distinguishes this from digital talk is the absence of emoticons and other symbols to express ideas and moods. On the webpage where this example appears the reader will find, however, images and the occasional video clip, features which have been found more in text than talk, though this is changing with the growing use and adaptability of talk in social media sites.

Digital texts are categorised in this book roughly according to genres and communities of practice. Chapter 2 will look at educational texts set in virtual learning environments (VLEs), as well as informal learning settings, such as Wikipedia. Following on from the digital talk and formats brought about by social media in Chapter 3, Chapter 4 will examine digital texts found in online news sites. Chapters 5, 6 and 7 look at creative writing online, by analysing digital texts used in the production of poetry and various forms of fiction. Chapter 8 concludes this book by looking at digital textuality in terms of genre and how digital communication has given rise to certain hybrid genres, along with the role it has played in language **superdiversity**.

> **Activity**
>
> We all have received some sort of spam into our email inboxes. Randomly choose a spam email and analyse the language which is used. Is it more digital talk or digital text? How does the email use the affordances of email technology?

Digital literacy

Barton and Lee (2013) note that two areas which have been researching writing online are linguistics and digital literacies and that these complement each other. Taking this view, and as a way of introduction to the book, here we will look at the ideas behind digital literacies and will return to them in the following chapters, in particular Chapter 2, where we examine learning online.

Historically, literacy was about schooling – the ability to read and write. But in the past 20 years this has changed with the development of NLS, which looks at literacy in terms of cultural practices and power relations. Here literacy is not so much about communication and schooling as it is about empowerment by engaging in literacy practices. For example, those who engage in journalistic writing hold the power and influence generated by the public media; those who have studied medicine or law hold power in terms of work relations and in their position in society. While it would be easy to say that literacy is empowering, it would be more accurate to say that certain literacies are empowering in certain cultural contexts.

NLS can be broken down into two broad categories: those focused on literacy as social practice; and those interested in new literacies, that is, digital literacy and the print literacy which has followed the advent of new media and technologies. These studies connect the spread of digital technologies and the changes to social practices which revolve around communication. As suggested, one of the interests of NLS scholars is the concept of multiliteracies which we all engage with. For instance, reading to follow instructions, such as a cooking recipe, which might involve rereading and checking information, is different from the reading used when studying a literary text. The same can be said for what is broadly referred to as digital literacy. There are different literacies when using computers for different purposes.

According to Wikipedia, which in itself is a testament of digital literacy, 'Digital literacy is the ability to locate, organize, understand, evaluate, and create information using digital technology. It involves a working knowledge of current high-technology, and an understanding of how it can be used. Digitally literate people can communicate and work more efficiently, especially with those who possess the same knowledge and skills'. This definition might raise as many questions as it intended to answer. Consider the following points:

1. If we cannot locate or understand something on the internet, does that mean we are not digitally literate? What about people engaged in social networking sites?

2. What does 'working knowledge' mean in the context of computers?

3. What is meant by 'current high-technology'? Does this include mobile phones and Kindles?

4. If digitally literate people can work more efficiently, are digital-based literacy practices about saving time and/or being more organised?

Another definition of digital literacy, which is perhaps more straightforward and encompasses the main ideas needed here, sees digital literacy as 'the ability to understand and use information in multiple formats from a wide range of sources when it is presented via computers' (Gilster, 1998). With this definition, it might be useful to think of digital literacy as developmental. For example, Martin (2009) says that there are three levels to digital literacy: digital competence, digital use and digital transformation. Digital competence accounts for skills, such as word processing, electronic communication, finding information on the web, processing digital images and so on. Digital use builds on competence and is embedded in a social activity, where other social, technical and professional expertise comes to play alongside digital competence. Digital transformation 'is achieved when the digital usages which have been developed enable innovation and creativity, and stimulate significant change within the professional or knowledge domain or the personal and social context. This change could happen at the individual level, or at that of the group or organisation' (Martin, 2009, p. 9). Digital transformation is becoming increasingly practised by those using the internet due to Web 2.0 technologies. Web 2.0 refers to online technologies with user-generated content, and the term is also used to refer to media sharing sites, blogs and wikis, as well as social networking sites (SNSs).

Here we have outlined the ideas of digital literacy as it is situated contextually as part of social practices. At the same time, digital literacy, as suggested by Gilster and Martin among others, involves certain skills and practices, such as how to use search engines and input images, in addition to those natural skills of speaking and writing practices. It also involves practices which differ from face-to-face conversation and writing in printed texts, such as the use of digital talk acronyms and editing digital texts.

Activity

Make a list of your literacy practices online over the past few days. Consider whether these involved working with digital talk or digital text (if you can make that distinction). How does this compare with face-to-face communication and/or writing without a computer?

Overview of critical approaches to digital textuality

The distinction made in this chapter between digital talk and digital text is useful for our purposes in that these different text types tend to be analysed using different approaches, much in the same way as linguists have different frameworks for analysing speech and writing. Uniting these different approaches are the ideas expressed above with NLS perspectives, where digital literacies are looked at through the lens of social practices in context.

When looking at digital talk, Discourse Analysis (DA), Conversational Analysis (CA) and Grice's Cooperative Principle are amongst the approaches to be applied. As we can see from the example of digital talk above, the taking of turns and some features of style are shared between such online communication and oral conversation, making such approaches reasonable. However, scholars are now asking if discourse in these new digital environments calls for new methods of analysis and new theoretical understandings. This point is worth considering as technological affordances of CMCs, such as multimodality and time lapses between turns, bear significantly upon analysis. Moreover, social context of CMCs, such as participants in different social and cultural environments communicating together, alongside the likely anonymity of some participants, places discourse in environments different from those originally examined by DA and CA theorists. Taking into account these differences between oral communication and CMC, we will draw from DA and CA as worthy starting points for analysis.

Discourse Analysis is a term sometimes used in a broad sense to cover all sorts of discourse analysis, including pragmatics and Conversational Analysis. In its stricter sense, it refers to a method of analysing spoken language and it relates primarily to identifying rules which speakers and listeners follow in order to produce coherent exchanges. Some studies within DA (such as Brown and Yule, 1983 and Johnstone, 2008) pay particularly close attention to the context of situation and the resulting structures of discourse; for example, studies on classroom discourse have noted patterns of discourse structures within, where teachers ask a question and students give answers, followed by the teacher's feedback to the answers (Sinclair and Coulthard, 1975). This simple example, of course, has many variations. We will also find discourse structures when we examine digital talk within specific social networking sites.

While DA is concerned with the structure of discourse, CA concerns itself more with the management of conversational discourse. This field of linguistics had its origins in sociology, with the works of Garfinkel (1967), and was further developed by Sacks (1992). With a social emphasis, factors emerge such as the interpersonal relationship between speakers and listeners and the ways in which conversations are constructed cooperatively by participants. We have already highlighted some of these features in our discussion of digital talk above and will return to these in upcoming chapters.

Grice's well-known Cooperative Principle also draws our attention to the way conversation is based on participants' cooperation in communication. Using **Grice's Maxims** we can consider ways in which meanings are implied in CMC. For instance, in the chat room above, KD in line 10 makes a comment about 'tipping' not just being 'for cows', which appears to break the maxims of Relation and Manner by not being relevant or clear in this part of the conversation. A meaning is implied by the double meaning of 'tipping', which is linked (albeit vaguely) to 'tipping' friends to join the party (with the abbreviation TP) and the tipping motion which a cow makes while grazing.

Early theorists of digital texts were particularly interested in fictional hypertexts, which we will discuss in Chapter 7. Bolter (2001), for instance, chose the writings of Barthes and Derrida to illuminate the workings of hypertexts as their work described texts made of many other texts; such multi-layered texts require more reader interaction than traditional texts, and thus the emphasis of these approaches was on stating that the reader makes the meanings of texts. But as more recent scholarship has noted, Barthes and Derrida's work was suitable for describing the emergence of digital texts, where such texts were still reflections of printed texts, organised in similar ways and using the written word as their primary mode. Non-fictional texts such as newsprint first drew the attention of theorists in media and communications studies, with an emphasis on online versions replacing the printed word. As we are moving further from the forms of printed text and as more multimodal resources are accessible, along with other user-generated content, more communication and linguistic-based theories come into play.

Current developments in linguistic analysis of online communication and digital texts have their roots in social semiotic approaches to language. Social semiotics is a framework of language study, which most brings together traditions in the Prague school of linguistics with M. A. K. Halliday's Systemic Functional Linguistics (SFL) (Halliday, 1978; Halliday and Matthiessen, 2004). In broad terms, social semiotics describes language from the viewpoint that it is used by people to make sense of their experiences and that the main function of language is 'meaning-making'. As such, meaning is understood to be socially constructed representations of the world and always reliant on context. Here we will draw mainly from the ideas found in SFL. At the foundation of Halliday's approach are three metafunctions of language, also referred to as 'meanings'; these metafunctions are: the **ideational**, **interpersonal** and **textual** meanings. In brief, the ideational meaning relates to the message and experience of communication; the interpersonal is to do with the construction of relationships between speaker and listener or writer and reader; and the textual function involves the organisation and presentation of texts.

Halliday's ideas derived from Malinowski (1923) and Firth (1957), both of whom emphasised the study of language in context, looking at context of situation and context of culture. Firth and his students developed Malinowski's concept of the context of situation, adopting the term 'register' to account for language which is related to a specific context of situation. Linguists who followed on from Firth in this vein, including Halliday, developed a more detailed description of register, devising three main categories: field, tenor and mode. While these categories have developed and their definitions vary slightly among linguists, here we are using these terms as they are generally understood as elements of ideational meaning (**field**), interpersonal meaning (**tenor**) and textual meaning (**mode**).

An offshoot of SFL is multimodal stylistics, which applies an SFL framework to images and the interaction between modes, such as written words and images. In this book we will draw primarily from the seminal work in this area, *Reading Images* (Kress and van Leeuwen, 2006). In this approach, signs, whether they be linguistic or non-linguistic, are critically studied with the understanding that social context is embedded in the function and use of signs.

While social semiotic approaches help us to analyse digital texts (and can be applied to digital talk), when it comes to digital literatures, other functions of language in use emerge for which other approaches can provide deeper, more-rounded analyses. In Chapter 5 we will use SFL as a framework to analyse the way digital poetry communicates, but we will also refer to terms found in literary stylistics to describe figurative uses of language; in social semiotic terms such language use can also be seen as exhibiting a 'poetic function', a concept from **Jakobson's functions of language** (1960). For our investigation of literary narrative produced through digital texts, again we will place these works into an SFL framework, but we will also apply an approach from cognitive linguistics. Cognitive approaches to texts focus on ways of reading through mental representations, in contrast to the tendency of literary stylistics, which traditionally focused on the writer. According to Steen (2003), such approaches 'enable the analyst to look through the language or the words on the page, to examine a number of different cognitive dimensions of text' (p. 81). The cognitive approach used in this book is Text World Theory (TWT), which, as we will see, is well suited to examining digital texts as it draws attention more to the reading experience than the writer's intended interpretation; this is particularly useful where many interpretations and different readers' experiences occur, as we with hypertext fictions, discussed in Chapter 7.

TWT was developed by Werth (1999) and was built upon earlier developments in stylistics and cognitive psychology which suggest that humans conceptualise language through mental representations. For Werth, conceptual space is modelled on physical space; with this in mind, he proposed three interconnected levels to describe the reception of narrative texts: **discourse world**, **text world** and sub-worlds. In brief, a discourse world accounts for the background knowledge and knowledge of the text shared between writer and reader. The text world is that which is created by the literary text, and within it are sub-worlds, which include flashbacks and the internal worlds of characters. This framework has since been refined by Gavins (2007) into a more context-sensitive approach which includes the actual world; moreover, Gavins has added the idea of world switches, which better describes text worlds within text worlds (this includes flashbacks), leaving sub-worlds, rephrased as '**modal worlds**', for the internal worlds of characters and narrators. We also follow Gavins' approach by employing SFL to describe linguistic features of texts which are linked to mental representations.

Using TWT, 'even the most abstract of texts must be mentally represented' (Werth, 1999, p. 8). As we will see in Chapters 6 and 7, the surrealistic nature of many digital literary texts also means that meanings are often inferred or hypothesised until the texts reveal more information for understanding, which they do for some readers, but perhaps not others. It is for this reason that we also turn to cognitive approaches which account for not only events within a text, but those which are unrealised, creating possible worlds.

As social semiotics is, broadly speaking, a sociocultural approach to language study, like other such works we will also refer to the work of Bakhtin (1981) and Fairclough (1992, 2001), among others, for useful concepts and terminology, some of which you will already be familiar with.

Conclusions

By way of introduction to this book, this chapter has provided some of the key terms used for the descriptions and analyses of digital textuality, along with an overview of past approaches and current ones, which will be used in the following chapters.

While we have taken the view that digital talk is different from digital texts in order to consider various approaches, the distinction is not always clear when interacting with digital communication. This interaction is at the heart of what has been referred to here as digital literacy. To understand this type of literacy practice, we have looked to various definitions of digital literacy along with the concepts of communities of practice and discourse communities, as these are essential to the sociocultural approach to language study taken by this book.

Sample project

Follow an online community for a week or so; this community could be your own network of Facebook friends, or a more strictly defined community, such as your classmates who share online course webpages with you. Note the following points:

- What shared interests do its members have?
- How does the register of that shared interest appear?
- What links does this community provide for its members?

Further reading

Barton, D. and Lee, C. (2013) *Language Online: Investigating Digital Texts and Practices*. Abingdon: Routledge.

This introductory text is good for anyone new to studying language in online contexts. It looks at online literacy practices, including multiple literacies and multimodality.

Bolter, J. D. (2001) *Writing Space: Computers, Hypertext and the Remediation of Print*. 2nd edn. Abingdon: Routledge.

Although some of the platforms discussed in this text may seem dated given the Web 2.0 platforms which followed this publication, it has interesting discussions on the shift in thinking from print to digital texts. It includes the early criticism and approaches to digital texts, in particular the work of Barthes and Derrida.

Clark, U. (2007) *Studying Language: English in Action*. Basingstoke: Palgrave Macmillan.

This book provides concise overviews of many of the theories and approaches introduced in this chapter. In particular, see Chapter 2 on pragmatics and Discourse Analysis and Chapter 4 on Critical Discourse Analysis (CDA), which includes applications of Halliday's SFL.

Goodman S., Lillis, T., Maybin, J. and Mercer, N. (eds) (2003) *Language, Literacy and Education: a Reader*. Staffordshire: Trentham Books.

This collection of scholarly articles has an apt section on multimodal communication, which includes digital literacy practices and researching online language using corpus linguistics.

Tannen, D. and Trester, A. M. (eds) (2013) *Discourse 2.0: Language and New Media*. Washington: Georgetown University Press.

In this collection of articles from the Georgetown University Roundtable, mostly approaches from sociolinguistics and discourse analysis are used to analyse online interaction, especially that found in social media such as Facebook and Twitter. The articles cover a wide range of topics, including identity online, politics and cultural communication.

Websites used in this chapter

The Buddha Smiled. (thebuddhasmiled.blogspot.co.uk)

Second Life, chat log. (http://www.secondlife.com)

2 Learning and Digital Textuality

Introduction

In this chapter we explore how language is used for formal and informal education in digital environments. We begin by revisiting the idea of digital literacy from Chapter 1 and adding to it the concepts of 'digital natives' and 'digital immigrants' (Prensky, 2001) as it applies to e-learning. Here we set the scene for linguistic analysis of learning with digital texts by looking at learning websites, with a focus on the textual meaning of language. While all three types of meanings operate simultaneously, this meaning is particularly useful as it represents elements which are worthy of comparison between digital learning and its counterparts in face-to-face situations and with paper-based texts. The textual meaning accounts for the ways in which texts are presented and arranged and how they cohere within themselves and in relation to their environment. This meaning is also an appropriate place to start when looking at digital learning environments as it can help to describe what learners first experience when entering these online spaces and how they are prompted to interact with these texts.

We will analyse digital talk related to learning by examining a case study of students' online discussions in a formal learning context. We will also look at an example of informal education with an example from Wikipedia, which is for the most part digital texts, but, as linguists, we will also consider the digital talk found on this website. Given the variety of digital talk and texts involved in learning online, in addition to applying SFL, we will also draw from concepts in DA and CA.

Upon completion of this chapter, you will have a clearer understanding of the relationship between digital literacy and education. You will be able to analyse a range of digital talk and text in online learning environments and platforms, applying linguistic perspectives and terminology.

Digital literacy and education

Given the ubiquity of digital literacy practices, it is no surprise that digital literacy has been playing an increasingly large role in education. One of the earliest theorists to expound on the importance of digital literacy in education was Marc Prensky, who coined the terms *digital natives* and *digital immigrants* (2001). Digital natives refer to people of a young generation who grew up with computers, whereas digital immigrants are those who did not grow up with this technology and have needed to learn about them by transferring skills, for instance from using a typewriter to using a computer. Prensky points out: 'Digital Immigrants learn – like all immigrants, some better than others – to adapt to their environment, they always retain, to some degree, their "accent," that is, their foot in the past' (p. 2). There has been much discussion of these ideas since they were first introduced. Scholars today point out that these distinctions overlook the experiences of older generations who might use the technology, but use it differently from younger users.

In terms of formal education, digital literacy practices take place in what are often referred to as e-learning and blended learning situations. Simply put, e-learning refers to learning which involves using computer technology. However, definitions of e-learning range from the use of any technology (including electronic whiteboards and mobile phones) to exclusively the use of computers in a classroom. Definitions also vary in terms of focus, from seeing e-learning as a process for delivering education more efficiently to a focus on changes in social practices as a result of technologies. The evolutionary process of e-learning is often traced back to correspondence study, with modes characterised by the mass media (for example, The Open University courses on television); from there, e-learning as a concept came in with synchronous technologies (for example, video and audio-conferencing) and computer conferencing. This phase was soon followed by the world wide web, resulting in a use of all technical dimensions in contemporary educational contexts. Current trends into research of e-learning practices see networking and social connectivity at its core. Hence, a narrower definition of e-learning comes from Meredith and Newton (2004), who define e-learning as 'learning facilitated by internet and www technologies, delivered via end-user computing, that creates connectivity between people and information and creates opportunities for social learning approaches' (p. 44). This definition provides the scope of e-learning considered in this book.

The term 'blended learning' refers to the conjunct use of different delivery modes; these include the more traditional print-based and face-to-face delivery, as well as e-learning. Given the role of NLS in the overall approach of this book, blended learning is of particular interest, as students who work together in face-to-face settings also have online interaction together. That is, they form a community of practice, with a mingling of social practices and collaborative learning along with individual learning. Studies of these communities of practice have shown that in addition to creating new knowledge and insight, in these environments the interplay between experienced members and newcomers is important for passing on knowledge as well. We will see some aspects of this when we look at an online discussion of students in a blended-learning environment later in this chapter.

Digital literacy in educational contexts, as with all digital literacy, includes the use of multimodal resources. Jewitt (2008), a prominent scholar of multimodality observed that 'how knowledge is represented, as well as the mode and media chosen, is a crucial aspect of knowledge construction, making the form of representation integral to meaning and learning more generally' (p. 241). In other words, the way something is represented contributes to both the content and how that content is learned. While multimodality is not new to education (consider picture books for language learning or diagrams used in science textbooks), its placement in our everyday lives and our literacy practices has become more prominent with digital media. Moreover, with digital media in our everyday lives, even for young children, the boundary between classroom and out-of-classroom learning and literacy practices becomes more porous. This is important to bear in mind as we look at formal and informal learning as well as the range of example texts below.

Research on e-learning and blended learning have tended to be within formal educational settings, yet informal education within digital literacy practices is probably more common. E-learning within informal education can be described as any type of online participation where learners are not enrolled and assessed, but where learning occurs nonetheless. Such learning could be active, for instance, individuals learning by writing or creating materials within discussion forums or social media. Other participation might be more passive, such as the gathering and reading of materials to learn more about a topic. Barton and Lee (2013) propose that people learn online by participating in online practices, reflecting upon their online participation and taking on new identities (p. 128). Taking this approach, much of what this book describes, including online news, fiction and poetry, could be treated as fostering online learning. While recognising the broad range of possibilities for learning online, the analyses below are restricted to resources and products of teaching and learning available to us in online texts. Further investigation could take place within the realm of educational studies, examining, for example, learner reflection and identity.

Activity

Consider the informal and formal online learning experiences you have had. Write down the ways in which the modes were interactive and compare them to the experiences of classmates or with friends outside of class.

Learning environments

In this section we will look at the ways in which learning environments, in both formal and informal educational settings, are designed to communicate and facilitate learning. At noted above, this will focus mainly on the textual meaning of language.

Learning with the aid of computer technologies can be dated back to the early days of computers in the 1960s, when companies developing computer technology hosted in-house training through individualised learning systems. Whilst, as we noted above, learning online can occur on many different platforms, including social networking sites and online news sites, when we talk about VLEs, we are referring to a specific kind of networked space. VLEs are internet or intranet (internal to one institution) sites designed in tandem with a course of study, where users require a password to enter. Today, many educational institutions across the world operate their own VLEs. Two of the best-known VLE platforms are Moodle and Blackboard, which are adapted by institutions and teachers for the specific needs of their courses. Typical features of VLEs are pages where teaching materials can be retrieved and where students upload their assessments, along with interactive spaces for wikis, blogs and discussion forums.

There are numerous websites for learning online which share features with VLEs and are open-access. Many of these sites are provided by educational institutions and private companies selling their courses and by governmental bodies providing information and skills training. For example, a website for history exam revision for secondary school students called 'School History' (http://www.schoolhistory.org) works in tandem with the National Curriculum for education in England and Wales. Such websites typically include interactive quizzes and games on subjects to help students remember content. In a typical activity, learners are asked to type in the empty boxes their notes to answer the question 'To what extent did the role of Government change during WW1?' Learners are helped by having the answer broken down into categories. They can also obtain clues for filling in the boxes by moving their cursor over the command 'Hover here for ideas'; key words to the answers appear and then disappear again with the movement of the cursor. If we consider the mode element of the textual meaning, we can analyse these texts as occurring at a point in a continuum along a spoken/written axis. For example, spoken texts and the digital talk we introduced in Chapter 1 show signs of high interactivity, while written texts (such as printed newspapers) display virtually no signs of interactivity. However, at the School History website, interactivity is apparent in the asking of questions, setting out of activities and other cues expecting input from participants. But unlike digital talk and spoken interaction, participants are not conversing back and forth with each other; rather the learner interacts with the texts.

Exploring the mode element of textual meaning further, we can consider how meanings are created by different modes and their arrangements. Bezemer and Kress (2008) describe a mode in learning as a 'socially and culturally shaped resource for making meaning. Image, writing, layout, speech, moving image are examples of modes, all used in learning resources' (Bezemer and Kress, 2008). With a text in a written mode, graphic resources such as font style, size and colour help to create meanings. Images, as a type of mode, imply meanings through the representation of framed spaces, sizes, colours and shapes. In the activities in the history revision website, meanings are created from written texts and the associations users have with the written words; however, in addition, meaning comes from the use of culturally recognised spider diagrams. These diagrams are set up in a way to situate the question at the centre, with spokes leading to the answers, which have been organised by category.

Another key feature in analysing the textual meaning is to consider the way in which the text is cohesive; this can be looked at linguistically within the categories of lexical **cohesion** and grammatical cohesion. Lexical cohesion can be identified in various ways: for example, the repetition across a text of a single word or phrase; through the use of synonyms, **hyponyms** and **metonyms**; and ordered series, such as the use of first, second and so on, or seasons to indicate a progression of time. Hyponym relationships are used throughout the School History website, where, for example, the First World War is broken down into parts, such as the cost of WW1 and the government's control of industry.

Grammatical cohesion most frequently occurs with linking brought on through pronoun references, as well as conjunctions and linking words, such as *however*, *furthermore* and *because*. The School History website frequently uses bullet points, which represent conjunctions, as if to say *and*.

Although we have focused on the textual meaning of a text in a learning environment, further SFL analysis would include the ideational and interpersonal meanings. The ideational meaning can be described as containing a **field**, which accounts for what the text is about. Determining the field of texts involves an analysis of lexical items, especially nouns, and a consideration of what semantic domains they belong to. Educational texts, offline or online, can be described by their academic discipline, which is a type of semantic domain, but they can also be described more specifically. In the School History website, the main field is a history revision exercise and within that more specifically different periods of history which focus on various issues, such as the role of the Government during WW1. For the interpersonal meaning of this text, the tenor might be described as a semi-formal register, such as that found in textbooks. In addition, there is a status relationship revealed in this text in the way the author(s) of the text is assumed to be informative and play the role of a teacher, while the reader/user of the text could be seen as the student.

> ### Activity
> Visit http://www.schoolhistory.org, which we discussed above, and compare it with the modes and textual arrangements for learnhistory.org.uk. Consider the similarities and differences in how cohesion and coherence is achieved in these two sites.

Students' online discussions

In Chapter 1 we looked at digital talk, such as chat rooms, where we could assume that the participants only knew each other online and not in the real world. In cases of distance learning courses, participants in digital talk are not likely to know each other outside of their online discussions; they might, however, have knowledge about each other's personal interests and lives from group activities intended to break the ice and foster collaborative learning. In cases of blended learning, participants know each other in the real world as they are in the same face-to-face classrooms. This has interesting implications for the analysis of interpersonal meaning of language and the tenor of the text. For instance, as we will see in the example described below, there is shared knowledge and experience among blended-learning participants which is revealed through the use of **intertextual** references and humour. Another noteworthy difference between this discussion and others referred to in this book is that here the number of participants is fixed, unlike the unlimited audience of the world wide web. Participants are not communicating to a large and unidentifiable audience. The other key characteristic of these conversations is that participants are working towards learning goals, as opposed to the more socially oriented leisurely pursuits of the environments referred to in Chapter 1. This feature of students' online discussions is described by Abu Bakar (2009), who categorises interactions in e-learning as consisting of three levels: conceptualisation (interacting with concepts), construction (interacting with tasks) and dialogue (interacting with people). In such learning environments we can assume that interacting with concepts and tasks could be seen as the main purposes in these online discussions.

In the example to follow, students were instructed to use the blog for posting their ideas for language projects, including the text types being examined and ideas about possible theoretical approaches used in their analyses. In other words, the field is controlled by the topic given to linguistics students in an online discussion assignment set in a blog of a VLE (described in Trimarco, 2012b), to which only students on the same course have access. The participants were 35 students in this group and the majority were female. The initial blogger is referred to as A. While students were writing to each other, they were aware of a teacher's presence; the teacher as moderator stepped in to add the occasional comment about the assignment or to settle a disagreement about whether the project idea was realistic for the project assignment.

> A: For my research project I am thinking of looking into 'The Language of the Beauty Industry' and in particular the wording used to market the products to the consumer. These words appear scientific and obviously very creative so the types of approaches that I am thinking of adopting are:-
> - Fairclough's Critical Discourse Analysis
> - Carter's Creativity Approach
> - Working with a Corpora
> - Interviews or a questionnaire recording friends and families responses and analysing whether they belief/understand the terminology used to advertise the products.

I would love to hear what you think of this idea and the approaches I am thinking of using.

> B: I think it sounds very interesting. Stuff like that is very interesting; like how I didn't think it was necessary to worry about enamel and plaque on a daily basis until Colgate told me I had to.

C: Hello A, beauty sounds like fun. Someone did their presentation on beauty in the first year so this would follow on. Look forward to hearing more.
D: I'm looking forward to hearing your approaches seem like the best ones to be using on this kind of subject. I'm looking forward to hearing your hypothesis.
E: Sounds like a good idea. Will we discover that the beauty industry is full of liars!!
F: Majority male then?
A: Hi. I am constructing a questionnaire as part of my project about the beauty industry and the language used within adverts. I will be needing some volunteers and just wondered if anyone was willing in the future to complete the questionnaire for me? I am currently looking for the age ranges of 15–19 and 20–39. Thanks.
G: Sorry A....would volunteer, but sadly out of your age ranges!!
D: I will complete one for you if you like:-)
B: I'll complete one too. The beauty industry is evil!!! ;)

By commenting on each other's postings, a conversation-like interaction has been created. Given the context of the blog assignment, students tended to only comment once to each other's blogs, and here only two participants other than the blogger leave two comments; both D and B comment on the initial posting and later when the blogger asks for volunteers for a survey. For the most part **adjacency pairs** of requests and responses or questions and answers occur between the blogger and the participants individually responding to the blogger. The only exception to this is when participant F makes a humorous remark about males being liars in response to E's comment, but in a way which adds information. We can also see information added to previous postings, where B gives an example about Colgate advertising; here the participant is staying within the field of language study, but extends the field to other advertising language which is not completely within the beauty industry. The field of these students' linguistic projects is also developed when the initial blogger introduces the idea of using a questionnaire.

With consideration of interpersonal function and the tenor of this interaction, we can observe an informal register throughout, which suggests friendliness amongst participants. The only possible exception to this is the use of bullet points in the initial blog, something which in other writing might be regarded as formal; here it might be judged as using the affordances of typewritten communication to provide a list, using bullets points. The tenor of this conversation is also marked in the use of humour in a few of the responses and through the use of emoticons. In these examples, emoticons were used as part of closures, which might be judged as fairly standard to online communication or they can be seen as stressing that what has just been written is not meant to be taken in any negative way, occurring when the writer wants to ensure offence is not taken or in order to be judged positively. Interestingly, the frowning face emoticon (☹) also appeared in other blogs in this study. In these cases it was used by students needing help with their project ideas; expressing the need for help with an emoticon could be seen as an expression of their own face, wanting pity (in a light-hearted way) or as a way of creating solidarity with others in a similar predicament. These examples might also be described using the concept of **face work,** where these emoticons perform positive face (i.e., expressing the desire to be liked) or negative face (i.e., expressing the desire of not imposing on others, as others are using their time to help with the research ideas). Such face work is integral to the polite way in which these discussions are conducted.

To describe the tenor of a text, we also look for language which reveals the relative status and social distance of the participants involved. Relative status covers the sense of equality and inequality amongst participants; in online learning, this could include how much the authors of a website possess expertise or authority on a particular subject. In online discussions, relative status can also be revealed by considering terms of address and who gets to choose the topic of conversation. In this case, the students were on a first name basis and sometimes refer to each other by name; this is being done perhaps to create solidarity since it would not be necessary as the blogging software automatically names who the author is for each post. The close social distance of these participants is also expressed, for example, by the personalisation of the postings; for example, participants B and G reveal some things about themselves in their postings. This stands in contrast to the related technique of deliberate impersonalisation which could be used to describe the tenor in the history revision website examined in the previous section, where the style of expression is semi-formal and the stance is more objective.

To conclude our look at the interpersonal meaning in this example of students' online discussions, we consider **modality**, which involves the way speakers and writers express attitudes, beliefs and evaluations. While there are several types of modality, here we will look at epistemic modality as it serves to highlight features of digital talk in learning contexts. Epistemic modality concerns the expression of certainty or uncertainty of statements. Typical examples include the use of 'it seems' for uncertainty and 'really' to express certainty, especially where a writer fears she is not being believed. Epistemic modality occurs in several places in our example of a student discussion; the initial blogger, A, uses the phrase 'I am thinking of' three times to show her lack of certainty about her proposed project. Many of the responses to A's initial posting use expressions of certainty about her proposal, such as in the phrase 'Stuff like that is very interesting'. Yet, other expressions in the responses have what would be considered medium modality, as in the use of 'sounds like'. There is also low modality, or uncertainty, present with occurrences of 'I think' and 'it seems'. These examples of medium and low modality could be a reflection of students' own uncertainty about ideas in linguistics, as they are still learning; furthermore, these students could in fact feel certain about some ideas, but not wish to appear so. Such uses of epistemic modality stand in contrast to the epistemic modality found in many non-educational blogs, for example, in news blogs where political stances are expressed with high epistemic modality.

The textual meaning in this example reveals how online discussions in e-learning environments can differ from other digital talk online. The initial blog is arranged in ways closer to digital text than talk with paragraph breaks and bullet points. The response comments display **cohesion** and **coherence** with the initial blog and with each other; this is particularly true, as noted above, where one comment adds to the content of a previous comment. There is clearly more cohesion and coherence in this example than we found in the example of a chat room in Chapter 1. Part of this difference is due to the asynchronous nature of the interaction, which allows participants time to write their comments. But this is also due to the somewhat formal learning environment, where students are aware of the need to stay on topic and that their instructor is reading their contributions.

> **Activity**
>
> Visit a discussion forum or blogs for students, which could be one which you participated in, and conduct your own analysis of a portion of that discussion. Consider where the interaction reveals positive face or negative face and how comments may be hedged. How do such interactions facilitate learning?

Wikipedia

In this section, we are going to look at Wikipedia, which provides an example of text designed for informal learning online. Wikipedia was started in 2000 and describes itself as 'a free encyclopedia that anyone can edit'. Since its inception, it has grown into one of the most widely read websites on the internet, with separate Wikipedias for over 287 languages and dialects. For our analysis, we are going to look at the main sections of the Wikipedia home page from 8 October 2013 (http://en.wikipedia.org/wiki/Main_Page). Linguistically, it is interesting as it uses the affordances of the technical environment to present an encyclopaedia containing hyperlinked texts and embedded images and videos from other media. In addition, unlike their printed counterparts (such as *Encyclopaedia Britannica*), Wikipedia texts reveal some of the collaborative processes and the content of drafts involved in constructing their written encyclopaedia entries. Analysing Wikipedia therefore involves examining digital talk as well as various genres of digital text.

A typical wiki has two different writing modes. The first is generally referred to as the document mode, where participants create collaboratively written texts which make up the encyclopaedic entry; this is the default document which users see when they look up a topic in Wikipedia. These texts evolve over time with multiple authors contributing original texts and editing each other's work. The second wiki writing mode is called a 'thread' mode, which is a type of discussion forum where participants post messages about the document text(s). In addition, there is a third strand of a typical wiki, which is generated by the wiki software whenever a participant saves a text or an edit in the document mode; such tracking is called 'View History' in Wikipedia, and in other VLEs it is simply a 'History' page; this is especially useful for teachers, as it allows updates to be monitored and student participation to be assessed.

Another feature of wikis is sometimes described as 'wiki syntax'; this refers to elements of formatting wiki content, such as style patterns in the use of bold, underlining and hyperlinked text. Such elements can be described as part of the textual meaning manifested in these texts as they help to arrange the content and contribute to the **cohesion** of its parts.

Starting with the textual meaning, on a typical Wikipedia main page we find that texts are arranged in sections, which are boxed and titled with 'From today's featured article' and 'Did you know…'. The left-hand margin serves as a navigational bar for this page and other parts of Wikipedia and is a typical convention of many webpages. Interestingly, by clicking on 'Current events' a text page comes up with an expanded version of the 'In the news' section of this main page; this **synonymous** relationship between the titles, 'Current events' and 'In the news', is one way of establishing cohesion across the various pages. On any Wikipedia main page, the featured article is placed just left of the navigation column, in a prominent position for reading first, as we read from left to right. The written text of the article is about Crow Dog, a Native American who was prosecuted and hanged in 1883. While the text itself has lexically cohesive devices, such as repetition of names and a chronology of events, cohesion is also to be found in the use of a photograph of Crow Dog, which is embedded in the text. Similarly, a photo is used in the next section, 'Did you know…', to provide more **coherence** to one of the trivial facts listed in the section; here, bullet points are used for each fact to show that they are separate subjects, joined only by the implied 'interesting trivia' in the section header. Other sections of this home page include 'In the news', which gives news headlines, and 'On this day…', which lists important historical events on 8 October in past years.

Of course, one of the most marked cohesive devices on any Wikipedia page, which distinguishes it from its print-based counterpart, is the use of hyperlinks. Each stretch of blue text acts as a signal to additional pages which are about the topic and can be seen as cohesively linking one part of the website to another. In the brief featured article on 8 October there were 13 hyperlinks, including one at the end, which links to a full version of the article on another page.

Consistent with encyclopaedias, there are many fields to be found in these pages – and even across this single main page – as different topics are written about. More helpful for analysing such a website is the interpersonal meaning, where we can consider the tenor of this document page as a whole, as it is consistent across sections and articles. Wikipedia follows the register of formality used in other encyclopaedias with **lexically dense** texts usually written in the third person, where verbs are often in passive constructions; for example, from the featured article, we have the following sentence, which has three passive verb forms: 'The Supreme Court held that unless <u>authorized by</u> Congress, federal courts had no jurisdiction to try cases where the offense had already <u>been tried by</u> the tribal council, and so Crow Dog <u>was released</u>'. Unlike other texts on this page, the 'Did you know…' title uses the second person pronoun in a way atypical of encyclopaedia genres. This might be seen as exploiting the less formal and interactive qualities of the internet, where information which might be regarded as 'trivial' is given the same attention as 'hard news'.

The tenor of these document pages also reflects the interpersonal relations between authors and readers. The more formal tone suggests the authors' authority as a whole. This is heightened by one of the linguistic constraints in the writing of Wikipedia entries, which can be found in the rules of Wikipedia, and that is the avoidance of weasel words. These are words as defined by Wikipedia as 'statements which appear to assert something but subtly imply something different, opposite, or stronger in the way they are made'; they include examples, such as 'some people say' and 'experts declare'. However, given that any reader can become an author for Wikipedia, the authority of authors is a much disputed point. Herring (2013, p. 15) describes Wikipedia as 'democratic and anarchic' at the same time. She notes that it is democratic because 'there is no central organization, and anyone can contribute to any part of the text'. It is also described as anarchic in the way that its content is unstable and always subjected to updates. In response to criticisms of Wikipedia for its inaccuracies and slanted coverage of topics, Myers (2010) sums up the principle behind the website: 'Wikipedia is based on the idea that it is better to say something roughly accurate, and have somebody else improve on it, than say nothing at all' (p. 150). But Myers also points out, perhaps more critically of the website: 'Hundreds of thousands of articles in

Wikipedia are stubs that sit there unedited from month to month; if no one checks them, there is no reason to have any faith in their content' (p. 142).

As mentioned above, tracking of Wikipedia entries is found in its 'View History' pages, showing the revisions between versions, with contributions and edits from any number of editors. Sometimes there is a brief comment with the edit, explaining why a change was made, for example, correcting a typo; otherwise the discussion of changes is left for the 'Talk' pages. These 'Talk' pages reveal a very different tenor from that found in the document pages. Consider the following exchange by two writers/editors about the issue of changes to the layout of the main Wikipedia page:

> A: **Comment.** Everything else is fine except I don't fancy the arrangement of the sections. '*In the news*' and '*On this day…*' are too far down, they should be right below TFA. '*Other areas of Wikipedia*' should be at the bottom right above '*Wikipedia's sister projects*,' like the way it was. [name withheld] 21:11, 20 September 2013 (UTC)
> B: Some thoughts:
> - Why is the discussion taking place here? Why do we have to start with one editor's 'single' proposal? (personally I don't like it.)
> - More importantly, why is redesigning always about rearranging elements? Why can't we try something totally new? (I don't understand for example why we must keep 'Welcome to Wikipedia'; that's so 90s.)
> - My personal proposal (which I suggested numerous times before) is to make the main page more like a newspaper without focusing on news: we need to have sections on politics, math, science, arts, sports, etc. Just like newspaper site, we can let a relevant Wikipedia project to manage a section; Wikipedia project math can decide what to put on the math section; maybe newly improved article. [name withheld] 11:38, 23 September 2013 (UTC)
>
> Source: Wikipedia, http://en.wikipedia.org/wiki/Main_Page

Both of these postings, as digital talk, are obviously more informal than the tenor of the document pages. The use of the first person in this exchange works to personalise ideas and marks the attitudinal modality found in both postings. Interestingly, the second posting uses bullet points, as we saw in the student blog, to list the points, creating subcategories within the field of the new arrangement of the Wikipedia document pages. The second poster also uses questions to express opinions, a technique common in online language, such as blogs and discussion groups, as a way of establishing a stance.

Wikis such as Wikipedia present different text types for analysis in the way that the construction of document pages are revealed with History and Talk pages, which are worthy of analysis in their own right. In addition, Wikipedia serves as an interesting example of online learning, as the contributors are learning from each other and their interaction; this could be said to display what Barton and Lee (2013) referred to as 'reflection on learning', where contributors reflect and allow for changes to their contributions.

Activity

Try conducting your own investigation of two other public wikis, such as Wikispaces and Wikiversity. Consider these points: How do features of textual meaning compare with those of Wikipedia? How does the context and implied purposes of these other wikis effect their modes and interpersonal styles of communication?

Conclusions

In this chapter, we have reviewed the idea of digital literacy by looking at the digital literacy involved in online learning. This has included consideration of formal and informal learning contexts and analyses of digital texts and talk in these learning environments. We have drawn our approach mainly from SFL in order to compare textual meanings in these example texts and to help our understanding of the ways learners interact with these texts and each other.

Learning online is developing rapidly and some of what has been presented in this chapter is likely to have been altered with new technologies by the time this book is published. We can, however, conclude by commenting on more general aspects of changes to education with these technologies. In blended learning contexts, students' uses of wikis and blogs in VLEs are proving successful in providing supplements to the traditional printed textbook, which could easily become out-of-date, especially in disciplines such as business and sciences. At the same time, online learning has moved beyond the institutional VLE to incorporating Web 2.0 technologies and the use of public sites, such as internet blogs, wikis, social bookmarking sites (which we will discuss in Chapter 3) and video-sharing sites.

Sample project

Informal learning online is vast, with some sites more explicitly pedagogical than others. One site which has drawn the attention of educators in recent years is the Khan Academy, an online learning resource made up of YouTube video clips, which provide explanations and activities across a wide range of subjects. Visit the Khan Academy (http://www.khanacademy.org) and list the ways in which it uses the affordances of the internet for teaching and learning. Then provide your own analysis of the field, tenor and mode of one of the lessons. Consider how this compares with those sites discussed in this chapter.

Further reading

There are many journals in education which include articles about e-learning. Two journals which are devoted to e-learning include: *The Journal of Distant Education* (available at http://www.jofde.ca/) and *E-learning Papers* (available at http://openeducationeuropa.eu/en/elearning_papers).

Andrews, R. and Haythornthwaite, C. (eds) (2007) *The SAGE Handbook of E-Learning Research.* London: Sage Publications.

This overview of e-learning research provides good definitions for a deeper understanding of this area of study. It also provides a basis for further investigations into digital learning, with the perspectives of key scholars in the field.

Barton, D. and Lee, C. (2013) *Language Online: Investigating Digital Texts and Practices.* Abingdon: Routledge.

This introductory book takes an NLS approach to online literacy practices, as in this textbook. It includes a chapter about online learning and another more specifically about language learning online.

Bennet, S., Maton, K. and Kervin, L. (2008) 'The "Digital Natives" Debate: A Critical Review of the Evidence', *British Journal of Educational Technology,* 39(5), pp. 775–786.

As its title suggests, this article examines Prensky's concepts of digital natives and digital migrants.

Butt, D., Fahey, R., Feez, S. and Yallop, C. (2001) *Using Functional Grammar: an Explorer's Guide,* (2nd edn). Sydney: National Centre for English Language Teaching and Research, Macquarie University.

Halliday's SFL is a complex system of analysing language in context. This textbook works with key ideas and provides useful examples.

Myers, G. (2010) *The Discourse of Blogs and Wikis.* London: Continuum.

This book devotes two chapters to analysing Wikipedia. One chapter focuses on the 'History' pages and the collaboration and text construction involved in creating the document pages. The other chapter looks at Wikipedia's 'Talk' pages, with attention drawn to argumentation on these pages.

Snyder, I. (ed.) (2002) *Silicon Literacies: Communication, Innovation and Education in the Electronic Age.* London: Routledge.

This collection of articles comes from an NLS perspective and looks at digital literacy practices. It considers the social, cultural and education impact of these new literacy practices.

Websites used in this chapter

School History, http://www.schoolhistory.co.uk

Wikipedia, http://en.wikipedia.org/wiki/Main_Page

3 Social Networking Sites

Introduction

The first chapter introduced the communicative features of synchronous and asynchronous interaction and ways of looking at online texts in terms of digital talk and digital text. We saw in Chapter 2 how these features come together in e-learning environments. In this chapter we focus on social networking sites (SNSs), such as Facebook and Twitter, and in doing so, we will examine elements of digital texts and digital talk which help to define and distinguish these from other online environments. As 'SNS afford a unique lens through which to examine human interaction and self-presentation online' (Carr, Schrock and Dauterman, 2012, p. 176), these platforms have been of great interest to scholars across the fields of media studies, sociology, and psychology, as well as linguistics. Here we will take into account the human interaction found in SNSs by revisiting the notion of discourse communities. From a linguistic perspective, self-presentation, also described as identity performance, is also explored in this chapter. Both the formation and participation in discourse communities and self-presentation can be seen as purposes for SNS communication and help to provide a framework from which to examine digital text and talk. In this chapter we will continue to draw from SFL, along with DA, CA and **Grice's Maxims**; in addition, we will look at qualitative and quantitative studies; though it needs to be said that quantitative studies are of relatively small cohorts given the vast amount of internet traffic producing millions of transactions across the globe daily.

Upon completion of this chapter, you will be able to analyse linguistic features which relate to discourse communities and self-presentation in SNSs. You will also be able to analyse various digital texts and digital talk of the types typically found in SNSs.

What are SNSs?

As SNSs are a type of social media, we begin by delineating these two terms, even though they are often used interchangeably. Social media is an umbrella term used to describe the means for interaction which involves creating and sharing information online, and this can include Wikipedia and YouTube. SNSs, on the other hand, refer to social media which involves not only the creation and sharing of information, but also the creation of user networks. At the heart of SNSs is the idea that users are linked to other users who are linked to other users and so on. As defined by Boyd and Ellison (2007), SNSs are web-based services which allow users to do the following:

1) create profiles which are either public or semi-public;
2) display connections which they have to other members of the social network;
3) find other users of the social network.

The assumed primary function of SNSs is to expand one's network. While this allows individuals to meet strangers online, studies have shown that most connections are made with people already known to the SNS users offline. Moreover, of nearly equal importance is the fact that these sites enable users to create and display their social networks, which plays roles in constructing individual and group identity.

It could be said that SNSs started in 1998 with the inception of Yahoo Groups. That was followed by the emergence of blogging sites, such as Blogger.com in 1999. The surge in SNSs came between 2003 and 2006, which saw the beginnings of MySpace, LinkedIn, Flickr, Facebook and Twitter. By 2013, Twitter had 500 million registered users and Facebook claimed that over 1 billion people used their site each month.

Upon joining some SNSs, users are prompted to identify others in the system with whom they already have a connection, often through their email contacts. Depending on the site, popular terms for these identified others include 'Friends', 'Contacts' and 'Links'. However, it should be noted that terms such as 'Friends' can be misleading; though initially designed for social relationships, companies and other organisations now use SNSs, stretching the meaning of friendship to cover business associates, customers and the competition. The differences between these different types of 'friendships' are often apparent by the different tenors of communication; for instance, the informality of registers is likely to differ between friends whom you actually know and those who see you as a potential customer. Most SNSs, such as Facebook and LinkedIn, require bi-directional confirmation for the relationship. The one-directional relationships, as seen in microblogging sites such as Twitter, are sometimes labelled as 'Fans' or 'Followers'. However, Facebook also has capacity for one-directional relationships, where public viewers, not necessarily friends or followers, can communicate their liking of status comments, photographs or other items placed on members' pages by clicking on the 'like' icon; and an example of this can be found on President Barack Obama's profile page on Facebook (https://www.facebook.com/barackobama/info). This example is also interesting in illustrating the nature of authorship of many Facebook pages. At the top of the page it reads: 'This page is run by Organizing for Action'. In other words, President Obama is not the actual author of this page, but a political action group has created this page as a way of promoting Barack Obama as an individual, and indirectly promoting his presidency. In this case, by clicking on the 'Like' icon, readers could be making a political statement of support for the president or they could be saying that they like the 'About' page.

While most studies of Facebook have found that its primary purpose is to maintain and re-establish social ties, other studies have shown that Facebook and similar SNSs afford means for individuals to regularly communicate with friends and acquaintances. This regular communication via Facebook takes on various forms, including instant messaging and leaving public messages on members' 'walls'. While other internet platforms, such as email and Skype (for live chat and video-conferencing), also enable users to regularly communicate, SNSs have become a platform preferred by many. The notable difference between these other internet platforms and SNSs in terms of their communication features is that SNSs offer personal interaction which can have potentially large public audiences, facilitating a type of eavesdropping. Here, the personal becomes public and has implications for self-presentation; such SNS communications will be examined later in the Presentation of the self section.

Another type of SNS is that which revolves around microblogging, yet still meets the three defining features of SNSs described by Boyd and Ellison above. At the time of writing, the two most popular microblogging SNSs are Twitter and Tumblr. Started in 2006, Twitter is based on creating microblogs, called 'tweets', of only 140 characters. Initially, this SNS used text only, where users responded to the prompt 'What are you doing?' Today this site includes the ability to import images, and users respond to the prompt 'Compose Tweet'. These changes to Twitter since its inception have helped the site to evolve into, amongst other things, a news source (as discussed in Chapter 4) and an advertising tool for companies, organisations and self-employed individuals. These uses have been brought about through the affordances of mass dissemination of a few quickly produced sentences with hyperlinks and images, along with the ability to 'retweet' incoming tweets to others across your network.

The constraints of the 140 character blog are also of interest to linguists. Azariah's (2012) study of travel writing blogs makes a useful comparison between travel-related tweets and the traditional holiday postcard. Messages written in postcards are essentially public, as anyone involved in their posting could read them, and they are written without much planning or thought. Moreover, these messages tend to describe activities and the surroundings, but are lacking in detail due to the textual constraints. Similarly, a message on Twitter is often composed with little planning, and is definitely public and lacking in details. Azariah also notes that tweets, like postcards, have a relational aspect to them and serve to strengthen bonds between people. Given other features of this SNS, such as searchable tags and ways of addressing tweets to individuals, we will be discussing Twitter again later in this chapter as discourse community and as digital talk.

As many SNSs are linked to blogs, it is worth making some introductory notes about these platforms, though they will be discussed more fully in Chapter 4 on digital news. Here we need to consider that, like SNSs, blogs can also be socially interactive with readers' comments and links to other blogs, making them similar to the networks created in SNSs. Furthermore, blogs often link to content created by their authors on other social media platforms. Tweets from Twitter can be accessed via websites or fed into websites and other SNSs, such as Facebook and Tumblr.

As we have noted, these sites are multimodal in their use of texts and images. While images can be uploaded from users' computers or mobile phones directly, a growing practice involves uploading images from photo/video-sharing SNSs, such as Flickr. These sites also operate independently of other SNSs. Slightly different in its orientation from the social media platforms already discussed, Flickr is based solely on images, referring to itself as an 'online management and sharing application'. Users of this site are encouraged to tell a story with their photos. Like other SNSs, users allow friends into their account, thus creating their own network. Flickr also uses the same linking and communicative mechanisms found in other social media, such as followers having space to make comments or being able to simply click on 'like', along with 'favourites' and 'tags', so that images could be searched across the web.

SNSs and discourse communities

In Chapter 1 the idea of discourse communities was introduced; here it is revisited to assist in the study of SNSs. As noted earlier, discourse communities are communities of individuals who share common interests and goals, communicating within an understood variety of language (such as a register) and within certain genres, referred to by Swales (1990) as 'communicative events.' Behind the concept of 'friends' and 'followers' is the notion of forming networks and participating in discourse communities. As communication styles differ from one SNS to another, participants interact in ways unique to SNSs. For example, in LinkedIn, many participants create profiles for career and professional reasons, making the network one of predominately account creators and their readers, with less on-going or digital talk interaction than is found in other SNSs. These account creators and readers are likely to share common interests through their careers and communicate within the same occupational register. Moreover, they are following the genre of writing profiles which follow the conventions used in LinkedIn.

Individuals using SNSs can also belong to other discourse communities through affiliations created with searches and also through groups created across the SNS. Zappavigna (2012) discusses the ways microbloggers mark or tag their discourse so that it could be searched by others. This is made possible by using a hashtag (#) followed by a keyword; this tags the tweet according to category and helps users to organise these microblogs, along with other web content. This practice started with computer programmers using the # sign to preface terms for HTML anchor points. These searches create strands of affiliation and conversation-like interactions. Zappavigna uses the more specific term 'ambient affiliation' to refer to 'virtual groupings afforded by features of electronic texts, such as metadata, [which] create alignments between people who have not necessarily directly interacted online' (p. 1). Such searchable talk is further described as a 'bonding strategy' and can be seen as constructing a type of discourse community.

In recent years, SNSs have been transformed from being the domain of the individual and their networks into group-affiliated sites, giving these sites another communicative function, that of group formation. For example, members of Facebook could join one of many Facebook reading groups. Members of such groups might not know each other offline but share in communicative acts and, in some cases, specific registers in ways to form online discourse communities. These groups help strangers to connect to others, based on their shared interests, political views or activities. In addition, some groups attract people based on broader categories, such as shared racial, sexual or religious identities.

While SNSs which facilitate discourse communities may be groups created within well-known generalists' SNSs, such as Facebook, others strictly cater for specific interests, as revealed in the sites' names; for example, Academia.edu is a site for academics to present themselves in their profession and to link with other academics with shared fields through groups within the SNS. There are even SNSs for dogs (Dogster) and cats (Catster), which are obviously produced and maintained by their owners (as noted in Boyd and Ellison, 2007).

> **Activity**
>
> Visit the Facebook page of a famous person, such as an actor or sportsperson. Consider the fields of the various texts and the talk on the page, along with the shared background knowledge between the page's writers and readers of the page. From this, can you identify discourse communities to which members of this network belong?

Presentation of the self

Unlike most of the other platforms and genres of digital texts described in this book, SNSs can offer linguists marked examples of how participants online present and identify themselves to others. Linguistic research of social media has drawn attention to self-presentation with analyses of online profiles, status updates, and self-presentation found in interactions created in comments and microblogs. Any one of these elements of SNSs might include visual elements such as photographs and background themes, as well as features such as lists of contacts and hashtags for searching. The idea of self-presentation through interaction with others has been attributed to Goffman (1959) and was adopted in research on SNSs some 50 years later.

While the concept of self-presentation can be similarly applied across various SNSs, the technical features of each SNS platform shapes the ways participants engage in self-presentation. In contrast to webpage authors, who may manipulate page design, fonts and other visual elements to create a certain impression of themselves online, different SNSs have their own templates which place sections of text boxes and visual elements in fixed locations. Regarding this aspect of SNS, it could be argued that textual meaning is in part communicated by the site designers. Another technical consideration relevant to self-presentation is the ease with which internet users can constantly update and alter their online profiles, along with the continuing identity construction formed over time from interactions found within SNS pages.

Technological affordances are just one of the elements which shape user practices of self-presentation. Other elements include social contexts and the communicative conventions of the SNS. In some SNSs, individuals typically use multiple discourses to reflect who they are, resulting in texts which are **heteroglossic**. Baym (2010) observes that in online language 'we blend and incorporate styles from conversations and writing with stylistic and formal elements of film, television, music videos, and photography, and other genres and practices' (p. 66). Such features draw from social contexts and SNS communicative conventions at the same time. An example of this can be found in examining just one Facebook page, for instance, one belonging to one of my former students. In addition to the student's photograph, which shows self-presentation as a young male who has a beard and moustache, it contains status updates in what Facebook calls a 'Timeline'. In another prefabricated box called 'Places' a Google Map appears with pinpoints and comments partially written by the SNS. At the time of writing, the Timeline had these three postings:

1. Ain't nothing like family.
2. And typing stuff in a Deep Southern drawl. =]
3. Quite simply the best thing that has ever happened ever. Oh Terry. [Followed by a YouTube clip of a man named Terry playing the drums with his muscles; the caption reads: 'Terry Crews and the Old Spice team deliver another hilarious commercial. This guy is the real deal!']

The first two postings play with different voices in a humorous way with reference to varieties of spoken language and the idea of digital talk; this example is revisited in Chapter 8 in a discussion of super-diversity in online language. The third posting continues within a humorous and friendly tenor and with a display of personal taste in humour; the caption in this posting provides another voice, which promotes the watching of the video clip. The Places box with a Google Map uses yet another voice in the comments next to each pinpoint. For example, '(student's name) was at O2 Academy Brixton and 9 other places'. This third person account has a different tenor and is somewhat detached and objective when compared with the Timeline postings written by the student himself. Nevertheless, these places help to express the Facebook user's identity.

In her study of Facebook status updates, Page (2011) observes one of the tendencies of these updates in terms of **face work**, which reflects self-presentation. Status updates tend to involve their audiences in ways which are face-enhancing for the writer, while at the same time avoiding writing anything which can be face-damaging for writer and audience. The three status updates in the example above follow these tendencies, with humour being face-enhancing for the writer, and with comments about family (presumably meant to be taken positively) and sharing a liking for a video clip in order to avoid face-damaging expression. This awareness of audience can also be described in terms of what Bakhtin called **dialogism**; that is, status updates are written with the expectation of responses. This aspect of producing status updates might be seen as encouraged by the SNS platforms, which typically evoke responses, whether in the form of 'likes' or comments.

Self-presentation is, of course, integral to the users' profiles displayed on SNSs. Various studies in sociolinguistics have been carried out on SNS profiles, also referred to as 'about me' sections. (DeAndrea, Shaw and Levine, 2010) analysed the 'about me' section of Facebook with an interest in independent and interdependent self-presentation from individuals belonging to different ethnic groups. Their analysis included word counts of personal pronouns (noting the occurrences of 'I' and 'we') and words which denoted social interaction, such as references to family, friends and religion. One of the results was surprising: in face-to-face communication studies, Asian speakers tend to show more interdependence than non-Asians by identifying themselves in relation to others; but in this Facebook study, Asian profiles revealed independent self-presentation. One possible interpretation offered is that 'Facebook diminishes the use of interdependent self-expression' (p. 438). To this, the authors add that Facebook was developed and first used by Americans, who typically produce more independent self-expression when using this SNS, and that it could have served as a model for other users. This suggests that the social context along with the SNS platform influences style and content of communication.

Fullwood et al. (2011) looked at the 'About Me' sections of MySpace pages held by men and women, comparing the linguistic features. Surprisingly, women used more swear words and references to taboo subjects, as well as using more slang, than men. Moreover, they used fewer hedges than men. In other words, both genders tended not to use linguistic features often identified with their genders. For these 'About Me' sections, expression could be summed up as displaying 'linguistic androgyny'. These and other such findings are socially significant, as SNS profiles are often regarded as a kind of social CV.

Also common to the self-presentation in social media profiles are expressions displaying one's tastes, whether it be for books, films, music and so on. Liu, Maes and Davenport (2006) examine the ways in which the displays of tastes constitute an alternative network structure, which they call a 'taste fabric'. We mentioned earlier that in the microblogging sites, such as Twitter and Tumblr, users can search tags, usually in the form of nouns, which indicate topics to reveal blogs which might display common interests; these bloggers could then be followed in order to establish shared tastes. Such digital literacy practices can help to form discourse communities, as well as communities of practice, and play a role in self-presentation.

Typically, SNS users post a profile picture and a short author description. As noted above with a Facebook example, such photos and images help to display identity. On many of the SNS pages researched for this book, profile pictures were not photos of the SNS user; instead the uploaded images included outdoor scenes, cartoon characters and book covers, all of which display some aspect of user identity. Independent travel bloggers often use the same photograph of themselves which they display on their blog profiles (Azariah, 2012). This extends the self as travel blogger to another platform and keeps it 'alive' for the audience. Similar cross-referencing can be found in profiles in other SNSs where logos from organisations (such as companies and universities) appear on individual profiles as well as the organisations' profiles in the SNSs and on their websites.

Here we have described self-presentation in SNSs, with a focus mainly on profile pages, considering uses of language and images. As noted earlier, self-presentation can also be found in interaction occurring in SNSs. Many of these interactions arise from status updates, where comments are added by friends and followers. Like the example of status updates described earlier, these interactions display identity in a variety of ways, including humour, expressions of tastes and the presence or absence of engendered language.

> ### Activity
>
> Visit any four SNSs, examining two individual and two group or company profile or 'About Me' sections, and consider the following questions:
>
> a. How would you characterise the profiles or 'about me' sections in terms of the types of language used? You might wish to consider tenor and types of verbs used.
> b. To what extent are these sections using the affordances of digital communication?

SNS: digital texts

While SNSs offer a range of digital text types, many of which are accessed through links to other sites, such as news sites and YouTube, here we will examine two types of digital texts which are characteristic of SNSs: status messages and tags. In the previous section we looked at status messages on a Facebook page as examples of self-presentation; here our focus is on the textuality of these messages and how they display linguistic meanings. Status messages are nearly always in the present tense as they are in response to questions set in SNS templates, such as 'What are you doing now?'. While the content can be as varied as life itself, ranging from the mundane to reactions to world events and personal crises, the limited word count and space available, as well as social contexts, tends to make these forms of writing **lexically dense**. Moreover, linguistic studies have revealed features common to these text types across a range of SNSs.

In Carr et al.'s (2012) study, which involved analysing over 200 status messages from a group of participants over a two-week period, the most frequently employed utterance types were expressive speech acts, such as 'I'm hoping I pass this exam – for a change'. In SFL terms, these most common types of messages could be described as having mental processing (such as *thinking* and *wishing*), as opposed to material processes (such as *running* and *making*). The second most frequent were assertives, which are statements of fact, which included material and sensory processes. Also present in the data were examples of directives (command forms, seeking that the receiver should do something) and commissives (committing to future action). Here quotations were treated as separate from speech acts. Given the nature of status updates, these findings might not be too surprising, but with the growing commercial uses of SNSs, further studies could reveal higher occurrences of directives – for example, messages which ask readers to 'buy' or 'visit' something or somewhere.

The status messages have also been described by linguists as the building of narratives. Page (2011) notes that status messages appear in episodic forms and develop over time into larger, rather than being discrete, narrative texts. Page also points out that narratives created in social media could be seen as filling in parts of a personal narrative, where much of the orientation – for example, the situational context – is shared background knowledge among followers and friends; this reflects what Page describes as 'embeddedness', the ways in which social media stories cannot be understood without reference to the contexts in which they are embedded. An example of this can be seen in this tweet by an academic working in the field of heritage and tourism:

> Heading to @NHM_London for a dad and lad half term trip out. No doubt we'll use our tried and tested family stroll thru at speed approach.

Keeping with the present tense convention of the microblog, this tweet can be seen as an embedded narrative, which belongs to the larger narrative of this academic's life. Followers of this Twitter account will know that it is written by the 'dad' and that 'NHM' refers to the Natural History Museum (which is directly addressed by its Twitter account name).

We have already mentioned tags and the role they play in building discourse communities through ambient affiliation. Here we will consider ways in which tags and collections of tags form a type of digital text found online and in a particular type of SNS, those referred to as social bookmarking sites, such as Diigo, Delicious and Pinterest. Social bookmarking refers to the online activity of bookmarking and tagging online content, which is then shared with others; unlike file-sharing systems, here it is not the content itself which is shared, but the information about the content and the link to the content. Hence, these SNSs can provide information and notes about the tagged content, as a way of sharing knowledge. The tagging itself, which employs keywords, does not usually follow any institutional system of tagging, such as the categorisation of information used by librarians. Instead, the tagging found in social bookmarking has been developed by internet users themselves, and for this reason a collection of such tagged data is referred to as a 'folksonomy', a combination of the words 'folk' and 'taxonomy'. The creation of tags and descriptions of information are yet another means of self-presentation, as these tags and information can say a great deal about the tastes and identities of their creators. These sites also follow the criteria of SNSs by having followers and places for profiles, and thus can establish networks of interaction typical of discourse communities.

According to Mathes (2004), an important aspect of a folksonomy is that it is made of terms in a 'flat namespace'. That is, they tend to not follow hierarchies or relationships whereby one term belongs above or under another. This is unlike formal taxonomies and classification systems where there are explicit relationships between terms. For this reason, folksonomies in SNSs are interesting to study as texts in their own right, as they reveal sense relationships which language users employ to relate terms to ideas and images. The problems inherent in an uncontrolled vocabulary lead to a number of limitations and weaknesses in folksonomies. For example, an ambiguity in tagging can emerge since users might apply the same tag in different ways.

While many social bookmarking systems are currently in use, here we will analyse one system in the framework of social semiotics. Delicious was founded in 2003 and describes itself as 'a social bookmarks manager'. Like other SNSs, its users have followers and can be followed by others, in this case in a one-directional way without needing to confirm followers. It is also linked with other SNSs, so that followers from one site can be linked with the activity of another SNS. Given the limits of this printed page, it is difficult to show the network of links any account holder's homepage could lead to. Furthermore, each hyperlink can lead to pages which communicate as multimodal digital texts, which can be studied in relation to the texts they are linked with, along with the network of followers who are sharing their links. We can, however, isolate tags and comments for analysis. In Table 3.1 there is a summary of results for a tag search on the tag 'digital-poetry' (using spaces between words is discouraged in this search engine). The comments which appear are from the first person to bookmark the link.

TABLE 3.1   SUMMARY OF A TAG SEARCH

Delicious Search on 'Digital Poetry' (personal account)

Link title	Tags	Comments
Digital Poetry	poetry, education, digitalpoetry, edtech, ED529, ED527, teaching, writing, digital-poetry	Being a kind of art, poetry eludes strict definitions. The very nature of art is to challenge thinking.... [copied from the website, along with images]
Diverging Digital Roads: poetry and e-books	e-book, e-books, poetry, ux, pw, kindle, Twitter, eprdctn, epoetry	[no comment]
Electronic Poetry Center Home Page	resources, poetry, poetry-festival, digital	SUNY Buffalo site academic, hard to find poetic works
Stan Brakhage: DOG STAR MAN – PRELUDE – YouTube	screen project, artist StanBrakhage, inspiration, film, Brakhage, youtube, experimental film, digital poetry, poetry	[no comment]
glia – neuronal jelly with network sauce – 2009	art, poetry, digital, newsmedia, video, artist, media, hypertext, designer, music	digital poetry & new media jelly- independent digital media art, interactive online literature, USB-key multimedia poet Jhave
Digital poetry – Wikipedia, the free encyclopedia	poetry, e-poetry, digital poetry, CD-Rom, technology, poem, hypermedia, e-literature, digitalstorytelling, words	[no comment]
jason.nelson's.digital. poetry.interfaces	poetry, inspiration, hypermedia, media, design, poesiadigital, netart, multi, poesiaconcreta	In the simplest terms Digital Poems are born from the combination of technology and poetry, with writers using all multi-media elements as critical texts. Sounds, images, movement, video, interface/interactivity and words are combined to create new poetic forms and experiences... [copied from the website, along with images]

As we can see, all of the tags are nouns or noun phrases, which is unsurprising as they categorise and name content. Across the tagged links, we can see textual cohesion with several **synonyms**, such as 'digital poetry', 'e-poetry' and 'poesiadigital'. This illustrates a common criticism of folksonomies, and that is the lack of systematic categorising. Most of the tags place the website link into a field or topic category, while others label the website for the media that it employs, such as 'film' and 'hypermedia'. The ambiguity in such tags lies in not knowing whether the websites being referred to are about poetry or have poems in them, or are a stand-alone poem. Another ambiguous tag is 'inspiration', which occurs twice in this list; it is unclear from the tag whether inspiration is a topic included in the website or the tagger found the website inspirational. Other tags have a more interpersonal function to them; for example, in the first link, the tags ED527 and ED529 refer to course numbers and are a way for other members on the same course to find what others have bookmarked and tagged. The tags 'ux' and 'pw' are internet slang meaning 'user experience' and 'pussy whipped' or 'password'; however, knowing the meanings of these abbreviations is unhelpful if one is trying to learn more about the website link.

The comments in these examples reveal, first of all, that there are no generic conventions to writing comments, with three of the first individuals to bookmark the links choosing to not leave comments at all. Two of the comments have been copied and pasted from the first pages of the linked websites and appear to act as some sort of summary. The two remaining comments are presented as fragment sentences which continue to summarise in the way tagging does, with the one comment including an evaluation of the site; these are similar to notes kept in traditionally printed forms and looked at in terms of their interpersonal function – they could be seen as notes to oneself, despite the public nature of the SNS.

Activity

Visit StumbleUpon (http://www.stumbleupon.com), a social bookmarking site, and sign up so that you can list your personal interests. From there, you can explore the site and follow sites which have been tagged for you.

> Choose a website in one of your areas of interest and consider aspects of the textual meaning. In what ways is there cohesion between the chosen site and others in your interest category? How are the elements of the website's home page arranged to cohere and to appeal to those interested in this area or field of interest?

SNS: digital talk

There are many ways in which digital talk takes place in SNSs. For example, commenting on others' profiles and status updates, which can lead to reciprocal turn-taking, has features of conversation. Below is an example from my own Facebook page of a conversation which took place over a period of two days (initials used instead of names and photos of participants have been removed):

> Hi P. Hope you are well. It would be lovely to meet for a coffee sometime to catchup. Let me know when you're in Ipswich next if you'd like to meet up. G. ☺
>
> Hi G. Are you around Friday? Or perhaps early next week? P.
> Hi. I'm around either of those days. What time were you thinking? G.
> How about Wed? P.
> Hi. 3.00 okay? G
> Great. Stop by the office. See you then. P

As we can see, the four turns follow conversational discourse in having **adjacency pairs**, the first being a request, followed by questions and answers. If we were to apply **Grice's Maxims**, we can clearly see that the cooperative principle is being followed, perhaps noting the conciseness appropriate for this context. The use of greetings and closures display an informal register and one more common to written correspondences. This tenor between spoken and written language can be commonly found in SNSs such as Facebook, MySpace and LinkedIn. It is also not unusual to find much briefer conversations, for example, where someone posts a new photo to their SNS page, which might be seen as the initial turn of the conversation. This might only receive 'likes', which are a type of response, or a brief comment, which then ends the conversation. In these examples, the conversations contain clear singular fields, but this might not be typical.

Microblogs, such as Twitter, however, have a very different conversational style. As tweets can come into one account from various people being followed within minutes of each other, a one-to-one conservation can in a sense be interrupted. For people following many other people, it can be difficult to follow a conversation-like discourse. That being said, Azariah (2012) points out three ways to have conversations in microblogs: (1) through following or being followed; (2) using hashtags to search topics indicated by Twitter users; and (3) using @ to address a particular user amongst followers for a personal conversation.

The first two ways tend to produce one-sided conversations. Through following or being followed, many one-sided conversations transpire where the follower is only reading the incoming tweets and not responding. Another type of one-sided conversation exists in the form of retweeting, that is, sending out a tweet you have received to your network of followers. While some might see retweeting as simply copying and rebroadcasting, studies have suggested that this practice encourages conversations which give rise to a sense of shared emotions, expressions and conversational contexts. It is no surprise that participants in Twitter want to be retweeted, especially celebrities, politicians and commercial retailers. Along these lines, Twitter as a 'crowdsourcing' mechanism involves retweets spreading across followers in order to get support for an idea or project.

In the second section we mentioned the use of hashtags to create an affiliation amongst microbloggers when tagged terms are searched. This too can be seen as a one-sided conversation in and of itself. However, it could be used to initiate following a tweeter and/or addressing another tweeter directly. For direct address in microblogs, bloggers use @ followed by the addressee's username; while the tweet is still public only one individual is being addressed.

Conversation can also be initiated by using questions. In his survey of SNSs, Ringel (2010, cited in Zappavigna, 2012) showed that recommendation and opinion questions were the most frequently asked types of questions. The tweets below are examples of conversation starters:

What are the implications for closure of Hadrian's Wall Trust for the newly developing heritage business models? #heritagefutures

Terry Moore: Why is 'x' the unknown? on.ted.com/eCjW#TED

The first tweet is an opinion question with a cross-referencing hashtag; those following this Twitter account would be aware of the plans to close the heritage trust. The second example makes a recommendation to the ted.com website, while also posing a question; there were five tweets directly responding to this one.

As a final point in this section, it needs to be noted that, like face-to-face conversation, Twitter conversations can be highly elliptical with shared context playing a key role in communication. Consider this tweet, supposedly from 'God', which appeared in the small hours of the morning following the announcement that President Barack Obama had been re-elected; the tweet simply read: 'You're welcome'. Anyone reading this much-retweeted tweet understood that this was an answer to the first part of an **adjacency pair** of someone saying 'Thank God' or 'Thank you, God'. Here elliptical discourse is used to comic effect.

> **Activity**
>
> If you do not have a Twitter account, create one at https://twitter.com/; otherwise, use your own account. Once you have started to follow other Tweeters, collect a page of ten tweets appearing together for an analysis. When examining these tweets, look for linguistic features shared with oral conversation, drawing from DA, CA and Grice's Maxims.

Conclusions

According to Boyd and Ellison (2007), 'social network sites are structured as personal (or "egocentric") networks, with the individual at the centre of their own community'. In this chapter we have discussed SNSs in the light of these characteristics by considering them as enabling discourse communities, on the one hand, while also being platforms for self-presentation. However, as SNSs have grown in popularity and changed in purpose since the time of Boyd and Ellison's research, we have also seen the formation of topic-centred communities and linking which goes beyond the self. Today, along with the multitude of special interest groups establishing their presence in SNSs, companies, universities and non-profit organisations have Facebook pages and use Twitter as standard practice.

As SNSs offer a wide range of genres of digital texts and digital talk, it is not possible to generalise about any type of SNS language or linguistic features. Here we have chosen examples of digital text and talk which are unique to these sites or exploit the affordances in interesting ways, and we have analysed them using the concepts and tools found in SFL, CA and DA. Our examination of SNSs does not completely end here; as we will see in the next chapter, tweets are commonly used to spread news across individuals and mainstream media.

Sample projects

1. Examine your own Facebook or Twitter account over an extended period of time (depending on how much you use the account) from the past and consider the following points:
    a. Have you created tags or followed tags? Do you feel you are part of an 'affiliated' group?
    b. Over time do your status updates or tweets create or fill in narratives of your life? Could you apply concepts from narrative analysis, such as **Labov's elements of oral narratives**?
2. Sites such as YouTube and TripAdvisor include many SNS functions, such as 'Like' icons and spaces for comments. Visit one of these sites and find a page with several comments about one subject, such as a video clip or holiday destination. Analyse these comments in terms of their interactivity as digital talk and the ways in which self-presentation is manifested.

Further reading

For academic research, you might wish to consider these journals*: Language at Internet* (open access: http://www.languageatinternet.org/) and *The Journal of Computer Mediated Communication.*

Barton, D. and Lee, C. (2013) *Language Online: Investigating Digital Texts and Practices*. Abingdon: Routledge.

This introductory linguistic text includes an investigation of Flickr, which is referred to in several places. This includes approaching the photo-sharing site in terms of stance-taking and communicating multimodally.

Page, R.E. (2012) *Stories and Social Media: Identities and Interaction.* London: Routledge.

Taking a sociolinguistics approach, this book looks at how creating texts and interaction in social media involve narratives and are important to creating identities for their creators and their audiences. SNSs which are examined include Twitter, Facebook, Tumblr, MySpace and Orkut.

Seargeant, P. and Tagg, C. (2014) *The Language of Social Media: Identity and Community on the Internet.* Basingstoke: Palgrave Macmillan

This collection of scholarly articles looks at the performance of social identities and the construction of communities in social media. With these approaches, SNS practices are investigated across a range of contexts, including students in Hong Kong and youth in Japan.

Tannen, D. and Trester, A. M. (eds) (2013) *Discourse 2.0: Language and New Media.* Washington: Georgetown University Press.

This collection of scholarly articles includes several studies analysing interaction and identity in SNSs. The approaches used are situated in sociolinguistics and DA.

Zappavigna, M. (2012) *Discourse of Twitter and Social Media.* London: Continuum.

Using a large Twitter corpus of over 100 million tweets, this book examines linguistic patterns found in this popular SNS. The concept of 'ambient affiliation' mentioned in this chapter is explored in detail, along with other topics, such as online humour.

Websites used in this chapter

Delicious, https://delicious.com

Facebook, https://www.facebook.com

LinkedIn, https://www.linkedin.com

Twitter, https://www.twitter.com

4 Digital News

Introduction

Maynard (2001) describes internet news as 'less a series of "discrete" meals…. Rather, it's a robust, all-day buffet, containing fast food, junk food, fine dining and everything in between' (p. 12). Anyone who has used the internet to obtain news can appreciate this metaphor, as online news can range from brief headlines to in-depth analysis and from the well-researched to the dubious. As a result, the internet has had a significant impact on journalism and the dissemination of news since the mid-1990s resulting in this 'all-day buffet'. In this chapter we explore ways in which news is communicated in the interactive setting of the internet by looking at news sites run by mainstream media (i.e., the printed press and television networks), as well as at sites which are unique products of the internet itself, namely news blogs. After introducing these different news formats and how they use the affordances of the internet, we will analyse these news sources collectively from the perspective of social semiotics, applying SFL and aspects of multimodal analysis, given that news in digital formats tends to be presented in multimodal texts. We continue with multimodal analysis in Chapter 5, where images tend to add independent meaning to texts, whereas here we are focusing on the relationship between words and images in news texts.

Upon completion of this chapter you will be able to approach analysing a range of digital texts conveying news items using semiotic approaches, along with drawing insights from other linguistic analyses. You will also have a deeper understanding of SNSs, as these sites have been integrated into the broader spectrum of digital news.

By way of introduction, here we will briefly consider linguistic approaches to the language and textual structures of news coverage by summarising the two predominant approaches: Critical Discourse Analysis (CDA) and Bell's schema of news narratives. CDA focuses on power in language use and how language reveals power relationships, in particular those power relationships occurring at social and institutional levels and the ways they create and perpetuate ideologies. When applied to texts from news genres, CDA highlights the ways language structures can be used to enable bias, which could stem from political, religious or social ideologies. Analysing sentences in this way, CDA has drawn from SFL and, in particular, from **transitivity** analysis, used to describe elements of the ideational meaning. For example, consider the headlines below about the same news story from 9 December 2013 taken from two different online mainstream news sites. Their first lines have been included below the headlines since they appeared that way on each website's main page and act as a second headline to entice readers to click onto the fuller version of the story.

> Kiev protesters topple Lenin statue
>
> Occupiers of City Hall defy threat of police action as report of secret Ukraine deal with Putin is denied
>
> (*The Guardian*)
>
> Statue of Lenin torn down in Kiev amid huge pro-EU protest
>
> Demonstrators smash statue of former Communist leader with hammers
>
> (*The Independent*)

The two headlines clearly depict the same event, the tearing down of the statue of Lenin. But in the main headline of the first example the actors of the clause are the protesters who carry out the process of toppling the Lenin statue (which is the goal). In the main headline of the second example, while the statue is still the target in this passive clause, it is torn down by unknown actors and appears to happen due to the circumstances, which are expressed as 'amid huge pro-EU protest'. Yet the second headline in this example from *The Independent* not only makes the protestors (here referred to as 'demonstrators') the actors of the process, the material process is 'smash' and the circumstance is 'with hammers'. This connotes a more violent depiction of events than those described in *The Guardian* example. Moreover, this first example refers to the demonstrators as 'occupiers of City Hall', which has associations with peaceful as well as violent protests. The second process in this *Guardian* example is 'defy', which depending on the context could be a material process if it involves doing a physical action or as a behavioural process where it accounts for states of consciousness. In a full CDA analysis, which would include the full articles as well as other texts from the same publications on this subject, these differences would be explored for their ideological foundations and reciprocally for their contributions to social and political ideologies.

Bell's analysis of news stories (1991) looks at news from a very different angle than CDA. Bell's work reveals many of the generic conventions of these texts and provides a framework for analysis which is sensitive to the production of news. Bell observes typical patterns in the presentation of narratives in news writing and builds on **Labov's elements of oral narratives** (Labov and Waletzky, 1967) to encapsulate these. In Bell's version of these elements, the components of news narratives are labelled as abstract, attribution, orientation and the story proper (also called episodes and events). Following Labov, the abstract is a summary of the story; for news stories, this often appears in the headline and could be repeated in the first line of the story through paraphrasing. The attribution, which does not appear in Labov's work, tells the reader the source of the report, usually the name of a journalist or news service (such as Reuters and Associated Press). The orientation accounts for background information for the story, such as the place, time and people involved. The episodes and events, as the label suggests, accounts for the actions and happenings of the story. Moreover, Bell noticed that new stories are never told in chronological order. This is because news stories tend to begin with an abstract, telling the reader the main point, which could be a story 'resolution', with the remaining story filling in the background and events leading up to the resolution. Bell also noted how the narrative of news stories is often broken, with the parts of the orientation being added into the story-telling at various points.

Following on from the work of Goffman (1981) and Bakhtin (1981), Bell has also investigated the ways in which news stories are authored. Goffman looked at the collaborative nature of news discourse and texts, which involve different participants, such as journalists, editors and printers. From Bakhtin, the idea of **heteroglossia** can be used to describe this collaboration in news production as drawing together many sources and the mixing of many voices into each news story. For example, a typical news story has the voice of the journalist; the quoted voices of witnesses, experts and authorities; the voices of editors and headlines writers; along with more subtle forms of utterances taken from another source, such as the borrowing of government phrasing when news has been adapted from government press releases. Related to heteroglossia is the concept of **intertextuality**. The borrowing of texts is essential to news reporting, especially when sudden events, such as bombings, occur and journalists are not likely to be at the scene. A considerable amount of news reporting comes from unacknowledged texts written by news agencies, press releases and official documents which have been adapted and embedded into a news text.

Both CDA and Bell's framework could be applied to news texts in digital versions in the same way that they have been applied to printed texts. But as we will see, the news articles on websites and blogs are only part of the communication of news.

Mainstream media

Print newspapers were among the early users of the internet, first reproducing articles directly from their papers into digital formats. It has often been said that the Clinton–Lewinsky scandal of the late 1990s is the event which marked the birth of online journalism (Lasica, 2003), as newsprint tried to compete with television for coverage of breaking news; this meant that articles could appear online as a story was developing, and would thus appear in several versions with perhaps only one version going into print. Although online versions of print newspapers are becoming more autonomous, these traditional sources of news still reflect the appearance and presentation of the news in the printed originals. For example, online newspapers use the large Gothic letters for their paper's name, along with tabs which divide their information according to the same sections found in their newsprint forms. *The Guardian* even allows readers to download a copy of the day's newspaper in its familiar print layout in a pdf file, whereby the reader is able to turn pages as if it were the printed copy.

At the same time, online newspapers use the affordances of the web environment to create reading experiences quite different from their paper counterparts. For example, these websites enable users to 'share' a news story on SNSs such as Facebook and Twitter, as well as email news items by just clicking an icon. This relationship is also reciprocal, with news coming into news sites from SNSs, emails and RSS feeds. *The Huffington Post,* which originated on the internet, interacts with SNSs in several ways. This website prominently displays news stories and commentary articles as 'blogs', with each blog being given its own 'likes', comments and links to popular SNSs. In addition to this, incoming information appears as a column devoted to 'Social News', which reproduces news stories as they appear on Twitter, YouTube and other social media. Other intertextuality at this site occurs with the embedding of video clips from other news sources, such as the BBC. Moreover, *Huffington Post* articles freely borrow information and opinions from SNSs, a practice which is growing in journalism across the internet and in print.

In response to what is sometimes called the 'blackmarket journalism' of news blogs, which we will discuss below, mainstream online publications started their own blogs (Robinson, 2006). These blogs are sometimes referred to as j-blogs, a short form of 'journalist's weblog'. Such blogs could be regarded as **genre** hybrids because they share generic conventions and communicative purposes of articles found in the printed press and blog entries at the same time. Similar to a commentary column found in the printed press, j-blogs offer opinions about current news stories, and as blogs entries appear daily in reverse order with fields for readers' comments. The appeal of j-blogs is that 'they allow the reader to see the journalist as a human being, connecting with them without the stiff, impersonal voice that turns so many young people off' (Robinson, 2006).

Some studies of online sites of print newspapers have shown that high levels of content overlap with their paper counterparts, despite the obvious differences of interactive features, such as comments and use of SNSs. A study conducted by Doudaki and Spyridou (2012) in Greece between 2009 and 2011 also showed that despite popular beliefs about online news being more opinion focused, at the end of the study the online servers had a slightly higher percentage of their news devoted to news reports, compared with their coverage of opinion and commentary type articles. Surprisingly, the print versions had more commentary/opinion items. One major difference between print and online news in this study was the use of attributions, with online news sources less likely to state the author of a written piece (whether news, commentary, sport or other article type).

Another mainstream news source, television news programmes, has also taken to the internet, moving from an audio/visual medium to one dominated by the written word. Typical features of TV news websites are news stories which follow a traditional news print story structure, register and style, which will be discussed below. A notable difference from the printed news in these television news stories is the appearance of shorter paragraphs, perhaps to be more aligned to the spoken presentation of news. Using the affordances of the internet, video clips and live-news feeds dominate these websites, along with links to related stories in their archives and interaction with SNSs. Sky News has places on its site for 'Your content/videos', where viewers can send photos and videos for public display, suggestive of citizen journalism.

> **Activity**
>
> Visit an online news site of a mainstream news organisation, such as *The Times* or *The Evening Standard*, either through an internet browser or through a mobile phone app. Consider ways in which the sites use the affordances of digital technology, making them different from their paper-based counterparts. Place this comparison in a table for easy reference..

News blogs

Although blogs first appeared in the 1990s, it was only after the events of 11 September 2009 that this form of internet writing spread rapidly. Gunter et al. (2009) explain that at that time 'there was unprecedented demand for up-to-the-minute information about the dramatic events of that day which even major news agencies' own web sites could not cope with'. It has also been observed that these blogs added a personal dimension to the reporting of tragic news, which readers and viewers sought. This tradition of mixing news with personal views and stories has remained in news blogs ever since.

While studies have shown that the majority of blogs on the internet are personal and diary-like, news blogs have had a significant presence. But it should be noted that neither personal blogs nor news blogs form distinct subgenres, as there is significant overlap; personal blogs might include news items of public interest, and news blogs are known for their inclusion of personal anecdotes and opinions. Here we will consider and compare features of blogs which appear in mainstream online news and those which are independent of mainstream news.

Common to all news blogs are features such as the reverse order of entries, with the most recent first; hyperlinks to other blogs and within the same blog page to earlier entries; comments from readers; and a sidebar, giving links to the blogger's favourite blogs (known as a 'blogroll'). For example, the entertainment news blog Deadline Hollywood (http://www.deadline.com/hollywood/) follows this format of reverse order of entries and it has a lengthy blogroll in the right column of its website which includes a financial feed from Yahoo, film adverts, links to Deadline Hollywood's own 'most commented' and 'most controversial' postings in the last two weeks, as well as links to the site's archives. Typical entries have hyperlinks to other blogs along with links to mainstream news. We might describe such features as generic conventions of these text types which are clearly using the affordances of the internet to add information and opinion through linking to other texts.

According to Herring et al. (2005), there are three basic types of blogs: filters, personal journals and notebooks. The content of filters is external to the blogger; for example, world events and stories from other websites. Personal journals are about the blogger's personal life and internal thoughts and feelings. Perhaps the most dominant blog type in terms of news coverage is the notebook, which may contain either external or personal content, often interwoven. The Deadline Hollywood blog is a team-written filter blog, reporting exclusively on events related to the entertainment industry. Examples of personal journals can be found by browsing blogs on sites such as Blogger.com.

Examples of notebook blogs include the j-blogs mentioned in the first section.

A similar way of categorising news blogs has emerged from Tremayne et al.'s (2006) study of bloggers reporting on the Iraq War of 2003 in which he observed different types of posts, or entries, within blogs. 'Surveillance' posts were defined as those alerting readers to something they might find useful or interesting on another news source, for which a link was usually provided. 'Opinion' posts were those expressing the blogger's opinion, while 'Reporting' posts consisted of those absent of opinion but containing original news content, first-person accounts, or evidence of research. 'Personal' posts were those describing aspects of the blogger's personal life and in which issue-oriented or current events-related content was absent. In Tremayne's study, the vast majority of blog postings (97 percent) were either opinion or surveillance, with opinion being the most common. Interestingly, only 2 percent of posts were categorised as original reporting. While war bloggers were not heavily involved in creating original reporting, they were linking to it. Half of all links in the sample went to online news stories and another 10 percent went to news editorials. This categorisation of news blogs draws attention to possible differences in the interpersonal meaning of these texts. Where the fields of different war blogs might be the same or similar on any given day, the ways in which they express their purposes and relationships to readers appear to vary.

It is widely noted that the main source of news on blogs is the mainstream media, with bloggers filtering stories for the public and offering their opinions on the stories themselves and on the media's coverage of the stories. Scholars of journalism have suggested that this relationship between bloggers and mainstream media has better enabled the spread of information from the media to the public. Moreover, the choice of news stories and the approach to presenting certain stories are increasingly influenced by bloggers who contribute to the process of opinion formation.

Although news blogs are predominantly made of entries akin to the length of most news articles or columns, as we noted above, microblogs have also contributed to news online. As a social media site, Twitter's 140-character tweets interact with mainstream news, providing commentary. But this site also has tweeters whose microblogs contain news stories in their own right. In the examples below, we can see embedded in the tweets headline-style text, which is **lexically dense** with few grammatical words and with elliptical phrases.

> CONFIRMED: No more gunfire heard in #Tripoli for now. Hospitals still in need of aid, death toll still unconfirmed. #Libya #Feb17
>
> (From the HERMES corpus of Twitter blogs)

We can also see in this example the use of hashtags for tweeters to search for tweets with these topics. The words chosen for tagging are specific place names and a date which could help those looking for news items.

Blogs of any type are highly **intertextual**. It is not unusual for users of SNSs to spread news or comment on news stories from mainstream sites by simply copying and pasting a headline and including a link to the news site. One interesting and blatant example of this practice can be found in the microblogging site Tumblr, where a blogger with the user name 'Story of Man' reproduces headlines which begin with 'man' or 'woman'. This criterion naturally generates human interest stories. The blogger either copies and pastes the original story abstract from the news site or provides a summary of his or her own. Below are two examples from the blogger's postings:

1. Man arrested after hiding meth in ice cream
   A sixty-year old man was arrested after a Spokane County Sheriff's Office deputy discovered a bag of meth hidden in a quart of ice cream in the man's car.
2. Man sues ex-wife over ugly daughter – and wins
   A man in China sued ex-wife for their 'unattractive' daughter and was awarded $120,000.

The first blog was taken directly from a *Spokesman Review* article (2 December 2013, no author attributed). The second blog borrowed the headline from *The Orlando Sentinel* (7 November 2013, Mat Mauney); the actual abstract from the original article was: 'A man in China sued his ex-wife over what he called an "incredibly ugly" baby girl and won a lawsuit for $120,000'. The change of adjective from 'incredibly ugly' to 'unattractive' could be seen as the blogger expressing an opinion on the original story and the 'man' involved. The other marked change from active to passive voice in the final clause brings in the verb 'awarded', which holds different connotations to 'won'.

Since the start of news blogging, there have been many debates over whether blogs will replace mainstream news, and much discussion about the credibility of news blogs. Myers comments: 'Blogs as news have all of the reach and immediacy of satellite television, with all of the unreliability of the web' (Myers, 2010, p. 115). Although studies have shown that more people are reading blogs because they are losing faith in mainstream news media, at the same time the growing number of qualified journalists joining the community of news bloggers has blurred the distinction between journalists and bloggers.

With this understanding of the textual features of blogs, including intertextuality, and the way personal blogs and news blogs interrelate, we can examine news online in the framework of SFL to gain a better understanding of how they communicate content within the affordances of current technology.

Ideational meaning in digital news

As we have said, the ideational meaning of texts, including images, reveals the content or message expressed. When examining mainstream media online, the ideational function by and large follows traditional news reporting as relaying information which is newsworthy and timely, with specific fields for each text. The first notable difference between print and television and their online counterparts lies in the large amounts of news made available by the latter and the ability to provide updates on stories as they happen. In addition to this, as mentioned above, content of online mainstream news can be enhanced by the use of j-blogs, comments from readers and viewers and feeds from social media sites and emails which could include first-hand accounts of events.

By definition, 'news' is about what is 'new', and timeliness is a key feature of news in all of its forms, whether print, television or online. It is part of what is being communicated in its broadest terms and can be treated as part of the ideational meaning of news. Bell (1991) highlighted the frequency of time adverbs in news stories, providing both orientation for stories and at the same time informing readers of the recentness, and consequently the importance, of each story. This can still be found in mainstream media today. In his study of blogs, Myers

(2010) notes the frequent use of time words, such as *now, just, this morning, today, yesterday* and *at the moment*. Moreover, in the case of blogs, whether in mainstream or independent sites, the sense of newness of information is enhanced by the order of entries, with the most recent first and the inclusion of an exact time each entry was posted.

Another feature of blogs which can be seen as revealing the ideational meaning is the way in which blogs give extra content through the use of hyperlinks. The main type of link is that which gives a mainstream news version of a story, often with expanded content. It can generally be said that linking to mainstream news is a way to add content, while at the same time it is seen as adding authenticity and veracity to blog content which has been reported. Other links can often be found linking to the blogger's own blog to show related stories or to other sites to provide background information about named persons, objects (such as products or specialist equipment) or locations.

Other elements of the ideational meaning can come from readers' and viewers' comments on stories, video clips and blogs. Generally, these remain within the same fields as the texts and images being commented on. Unsurprisingly, comments tend to contain personal perspectives and beliefs, as well as anecdotal evidence, supporting or refuting the blog entry. The examples below are comments from a news story in *The Guardian* (Treanor, 2013) about the high salaries given out to bank staff during an economic recession:

1. There really is no honour among thieves.
2. Just another day in the office for the higher echelons of the detached banking world.... Detached from the real economy, detached from the rules of capitalism, detached from reality.

Both of these comments are personal perspectives which do not dispute the content of the original article. Other comments, among the nearly 500 which appeared in the two days following this online publication, were views about the Chancellor of the Exchequer, George Osborne, and the unemployment rates in the UK, which are clearly related content. But other comments introduced new fields with comments about, for example, the abolition of slavery.

Ideational meaning also emerges from the use of images, and given the abundance of images in online news, it is worth considering these representations of meaning. Although Halliday originally formulated this metafunction for linguistic structures, Kress and van Leeuwen (2006) have applied them to the detailed analysis of images. In keeping with Halliday's notion of transitivity, which is linked to ideational meaning, ideas in a text are presented in terms of participants, processes and circumstances. For instance, a photo from the sports pages of a news site might show two cricketers (the participants) running (the process) during a test cricket match (the circumstance). Kress and van Leeuwen suggest that these representations follow two patterns, presentational and conceptual. **Presentational patterns** refer to the participants as belonging to a narrative. **Conceptual patterns** refer to participants' generalised characteristics, such as class, age and social significance. In the example of a sports page photo, the presentational pattern is manifested in the two participants being part of the narrative of a game of cricket taking place, and the conceptual patterns which they display could include their roles as players and the countries they represent. In news stories in general, presentational patterns tend to cohere with the story in the written text and could be seen as offering clarity for readers. Conceptual patterns, on the other hand, can be used to express characteristics which are not necessarily present in the written text. For example, a news story about an alleged suspect being arrested could describe the narrative events of the arrest with background information pertaining to time and place without direct mention of the suspect's race or social class; yet these conceptual patterns may be displayed or implied in the photograph which accompanies the text. These meanings are important to consider for news reading where readers also tend to skim pages looking for information quickly.

> **Activity**
>
> Go to any news site and analyse the multimodality of the site. Identify the representational and conceptual patterns in the images. To what extent do the images cohere with the texts?

Interpersonal meaning in digital news

While there are many aspects of the interpersonal meaning which can be explored in the communication of news, we are focusing here on two aspects which appear salient in the environment of the internet, namely **register** and **modality**. Within these elements we will see distinctions between mainstream news and news blogs, along with variation across news genres.

Register in news texts is multifaceted and far from straightforward. News reporting of current events, for example, has traditionally used a somewhat formal register in order to display an objective tone desirable in this genre. The opinions and commentaries in newspapers, however, have been more prone to informality. The register found in tabloid commentaries, for instance, has been known for its use of colloquialism, fragmented sentences, questions and varied typography in order to mimic speech in written texts (Fowler, 1991). News reporting in mainstream media has continued to employ a formal register, whereas j-blogs and independent news blogs have employed a mix of formal and informal registers. Consider the examples below; the first is a j-blog from *The Daily Telegraph* and the second from an independent news blog.

1. Every parent knows how easy it is: children have a magnetic attraction to anything with a screen, and an uncanny way of squirreling phones and iPads away when you're [sic] back is turned. And they seem to have been hard-wired with all the skills they need to pick up any piece of technology and start playing a game on it. There but for the grace of God, eh, mums and dads? Maybe. But the question that's bothering me is the one that nobody seems to be asking. What was a five-year-old doing playing a game called Zombies vs Ninjas in the first place? (From 'Children are having their imaginations destroyed by iPads and video games' by Jake Wallis Simons, 3 March 2013.)

2. It's hard enough to explain that you're a victim of gun violence under the best of circumstances. Most people respond awkwardly (if they acknowledge it at all) or gift me with some awful conspiracy-theory political commentary that's worse than Facebook sabre-rattling. At least this time around, no one has suggested to my face that I arm myself. But the get-yourself-a-gun discussion was easy compared with the one I have to have now. Now people fixate on the fact that I'm a victim of gun violence *and* that I make video games for a living. (From 'I'm a Victim of Gun Violence. I'm Also a Video Game Developer' by Carla Engelbrecht Fisher, 28 February, 2013.)

Both examples illustrate informality in their use of contractions, such as *that's* and *it's,* and phrases which mimic speech, such as *eh* and the use of parenthesis as if saying something in a different tone of voice. Myers (2010) has observed these and other informal features in blogs, noting how blogs can enact conversational interaction with the use of questions, as in the first example above, and that 'conversational self-interruption runs through a lot of blog style' (p. 85); this can be found in the first example, where the writer seems to go off on a tangent before getting to what really bothers him.

Register in news texts, whether print or online, can account for the use of specialist terms or jargon in some types of news texts, for example, those found in the business and technology sections. While the occurrence of specialised registers appears in online texts as it would in printed editions, there is one noteworthy difference. Texts using specialist registers online can provide background information through links to help make the terms less exclusive, though specialist vocabulary still occurs without links or explanation as a certain readership is assumed. For example, an article about mobile apps which teach children coding found in the technology section of *The Guardian* online (9 December 2013) has hyperlinks to a few previous articles on the subject, along with links to the webpages of the apps referred to. But what the article does not have are links to explanations of what coding is, as it assumes its readers already have this knowledge.

Looking at the interpersonal meaning of language also draws our attention to modality, which is useful when considering the ways in which blogs take a stance. In his analysis of blogs, Myers (2010) describes the three categories of stance: epistemic, attitudinal and stylistic. Epistemic stances reflect epistemic modality and concern the marking of certainty or uncertainty of statements. For example, using 'it seems' for uncertainty and 'really' to express certainty, especially where writers fear they are not being believed. According to Myers, epistemic markers are 'very important because they effect the way blogs are interpreted as part of news and political discussion' (p. 97). In the j-blog from *The Daily Telegraph*, 'seems' is used as a hedge in the phrase 'the question that nobody seems to be asking'. This hedging softens the statement to make it sound less pejorative.

Attitudinal stances involve expressions of a writer's 'personal aesthetic preference, moral judgement or emotional responses' (Myers,

2010, p. 98). In Myers's data, the most common marker of attitudinal stance was unsurprisingly 'I think', followed by a clause complement; for example, 'I think this situation has to stop'. Myers also observed weaker versions of 'I think' in the use of 'I suppose', 'I guess' and 'I suspect' (pp. 100–101). In both the examples above, we can see moral judgements and emotional responses in abundance, revealed through expressions such as, 'but for the grace of God' and 'the question that's bothering me', and the use of adjectives in the phrases 'hard enough' and 'some awful conspiracy-theory political commentary'.

Stylistic stances reflect the way something is said. In speech, this is reflected in intonation, pitch of voice and other prosodic features. In written language, this could broadly be described in terms of tone. In both of the examples of blogs above, choices of wording and hyperbole add a slightly comic tone to each piece. Myers's examples of stylistic stance markers in blogs include 'seriously', 'frankly', 'honestly' and the use of emoticons (2010, p. 99); it should be noted, however, that in the blogs examined for this book, emoticons only occurred in the comments to blogs and not the blogs themselves.

Images used in news reporting also express interpersonal meaning. For example, close-up shots of subjects are intended to be more intimate than photographs shot at a distance. Scholars have observed that in news reporting, well-known figures, such as leaders of countries, tend to be shown more in close-up shots, as a way of creating a sense of intimacy between viewer and image. We will discuss the interpersonal meanings displayed in images further in the next chapter, where they are salient in analysing most types of digital poetry.

Activity

Visit these j-blogs and analyse a single posting from each in terms of their modality and the way stance is marked.

http://blogs.telegraph.co.uk/news/author/jamesdelingpole/

http://blogs.channel4.com/snowblog/

http://blogs.independent.co.uk/category/the-money-blog/

Textual meaning in digital news

The organisation of texts and how they cohere internally and in relation to other texts on the same website can be viewed as revealing aspects of the textual meaning. In discussing Bell's framework for analysing news stories earlier, we were looking at aspects of the textual meaning as described in terms of narrative elements. A similar observation of the organisation of elements in news texts can also be found in what journalists refer to as the 'inverted pyramid' in news writing. The inverted pyramid stresses that the most important points come first, followed by less important ones and ending with the least important. Both Bell's analysis and ideas from journalism, such as the inverted pyramid, can be applied to mainstream online news as well as news blogs. Some studies have shown that 'even though weblogs could present an open journalism with possibility for multi-vocality and authority, they did not' (Robinson, 2006). The 'inverted pyramid' news article still dominated the writing of news bloggers.

While organisational patterns of news writing have altered little across print and online forms, whether mainstream or independent, as mentioned above, online news uses the affordances of the internet to link their news items to other texts and sites. Such linking could be treated as displaying the textual function of language, the aspect of arranging elements of texts to suggest cohesive links. In mainstream media sites, reading a current news story often shows links to past and related stories on the same subject, with one text acting as a reference to another. These other stories are signalled in a sidebar listing hyperlinks which are typically named with the headlines of the linked texts or images. This is illustrated in Table 4.1.

In news blogs, linking can appear in various arrangements. With the exception of blogrolls of the blogger's favourite blogs, links to other news stories and related items providing evidence, as noted above, tend to occur within the texts of blogs. Moreover, the linking words or phrases tend not to be headlines or titles of images. Using the same two stories mentioned above, we can see the linking differences in the sample news blogs in Table 4.2.

These tables also show us that mainstream news tends to have more explicit links from one story to the next, where the link name is a clear sign of the linked text. Tremayne et al. (2006) found that editors of

72 DIGITAL TEXTUALITY

TABLE 4.1 HYPERLINKS IN MAINSTREAM MEDIA SITESS

Main Story Headline	Hyperlinked headlines/titles
Oscar Pistorius due in court to face murder charge (*The Guardian*, 15 February 2013)	The golden boy with an edge of steel
	Friends in shock at loss of 'sweetest, kindest soul'
	Oscar Pistorius's life and career – in pictures (with a camera icon)
	Fear and self-arming in South Africa
	Justice Malala: our flawed hero has fallen
Demolition begins at home where sinkhole swallowed Florida man (*The Chicago Tribune*, 3 March 2013)	Raw video: Demolition of sinkhole house
	Photos: Man vanishes in sinkhole
	Photos: Famous 1981 Florida sinkhole
	How Florida sinkholes form

TABLE 4.2 HYPERLINKS IN NEWS BLOGS

Main Story Headline	Hyperlinked headlines/titles
Oscar Pistorius Nike ad takes on new, chilling resonance after tragedy [Yahoo blogger, Jay Busbee]	Jay *Busbee* [link to the author's sports news blog]
	Fourth-Place Medal [link to an award-winning blog by the same author]
	arrested Olympic sprinter Oscar Pistorius on suspicion of murder [link to the story from the day before from the official Yahoo sports page; the title of this article is 'Oscar Pistorius charged with murder, reportedly had firearms at home to allay fears of invasion']
	as SB Nation notes [link to a blog on a sports blogging website]
Florida sinkhole opens up, swallows man [Amanda Crum, WebProNews blogging site]	Amanda Crum [link to other posts by this writer]
	Jeremy said [link to a *USA Today* news story]
	Jessica Demico said [link to a Huffington Post news story]

news websites used links to provide context to certain types of stories: 'This pattern of choices resulted in the typical distribution of links in a network: A few stories were heavily linked, while the great majority of stories had very few links' (p. 293). In our examples, the bloggers' links include links to their main blog pages, which include profiles.

Other features of the textual meaning can be found in the display of social media icons, which tend to frame pages of news stories or blogs by being in a sidebar, along the top of a page or at the bottom. These icons tend to be small, but are easily recognisable. Their being positioned off to the side or corner of webpages suggests tagging and sharing as secondary to the reading and viewing of actual stories.

The placement of images is also important to the telling of news. Studies in multimodality and journalism have revealed the tendency to place photos which are not integral to the newness of a story to the left of the written text containing the story. This is because in Western culture reading occurs from left to right. So, what is positioned on the left is viewed first and can be seen as 'given' information; the text is positioned on the right side and is considered to be 'new' information.

> **Activity**
>
> Visit a mainstream news site or a news blog and read one story or blog entry. Describe features of textual meaning, considering the use and arrangements of links, social media icons and feeds and images. You may wish to summarise your findings in a table.

Conclusions

In this chapter we have built upon other linguistic approaches to news writing by applying SFL to the way news is generally communicated online. Along with pointing out textual features which distinguish online from print, we have also looked at distinguishing features of independent news blogs from mainstream online news. It is quite obvious that the concept of the blog, whether j-blog or independent, and the integration of social media into news sites are two of the most dominant ways digital technology has changed the communication of news. Both platforms have also given rise to citizen journalism, which is a much-debated topic in the fields of journalism and media studies. While many claim that blogs and social media have democratised the news, giving everyone access to deciding what is news and how to disseminate it, others believe the integrity of news has been lost with these developments.

Although not covered in this chapter, video clips embedded in online news sites also provide a wealth of data for linguistic analysis. In particular, as we noted with still images above, the relationship between written words and video can be explored as an area of further research which draws from the affordances of digital communication.

Sample projects

1. Visit a mainstream news website from a television network, such as the BBC or Sky. Create a screen shot of the main page (Ctrl+PrtSc) so that you can analyse a page without it changing with updates. Consider the following questions:
    a. What fields can you identify on this one page?
    b. Read the summaries of a few of the articles. How would you describe the tenor of these articles, and are they all similar in terms of tenor?
    c. What modes are being used on this page?
    d. For texts in the written mode, consider the occurrences of grammatical and lexical cohesion. Which type of cohesion would you say is more dominant?
2. Become a Follower of a Twitter account for a news site, or section of a news site, such as sports. After you have collected several tweets, consider the linguistic features of these microblogs; to what extent are they following the conventions of social media (for example, using hashtags and hyperlinks), and to what extent are they typical of news writing (for example, are these headlines and abstracts?).

Further reading

While there are many scholarly journals in the fields of journalism and media studies which address issues related to online news, most of these are not intended for linguists; however, in *Journalism Studies*' special issue 'The Future of Newspapers'

(2008) you will find articles comparing online and print news which are relevant to sociocultural approaches (available at http://www.tandfonline.com). For linguistic approaches, *Discourse and Society* (available at: http://das.sagepub.com/) is a scholarly journal edited by Teun Van Dijk and publishes articles in CDA and other sociocultural approaches to language study; analyses of news media are regularly featured.

Allen, S. (2006) *Online News.* Maidenhead: Open University Press.

Although this book is not intended for students of linguistics, it looks at the rise and development of online news. More importantly, it analyses the different ways in which online news communicates major news events, including citizen journalism.

Bell, A. (1991) *The Language of News Media.* Oxford: Blackwell.

Allan Bell is a linguist and a journalist who draws from both fields in this analysis of the language of the news media. As we have seen in the introduction to this chapter, his approach is based in the frameworks of sociolinguistics and discourse analysis.

Conboy, M. (2007) *The Language of the News.* London: Routledge.

This introductory linguistics book investigates the conventions of language used in newspapers, using examples from UK, US and Australian newspapers. This book includes discussions on identity and how language is used to construct audiences.

Fairclough, N. (2001) (2nd edn) *Language and Power.* Harlow: Pearson.

This seminal work looks at the creation of social discourses, with analyses of examples from news media. In this second edition, the internet is discussed as a source for social and political mobilisation.

Websites used in this chapter

Busbee, J. Yahoo Sports Blogger, http://sports.yahoo.com/blogs/

Crum, A. News Blogger, http://www.webpronews.com/

The Chicago Tribune, http://www.chicagotribune.com/

The Guardian, http://www.theguardian.com/uk

The Independent, http://www.independent.co.uk/

Tumblr, http://www.tumblr.com/

5 Digital Poetry

Introduction

Digital poetry, or e-poetry as it is also called, basically refers to poetic texts produced and read via a computer. Interestingly, when the Web started to become popular, a mass output of poetry appeared online, but this poetry did little to use the affordances of the new media. Instead, poetry was reproduced as if photocopied from the printed page and nothing more. But this has certainly changed with the use of image montages and Flash (a multimedia software platform for creating graphics and animation), along with hyperlink coding. With digital mediation, poems can also be interactive, allowing readers to take the poems at their own pace, or animated in ways closer to films.

According to Funkhouser (2012), 'Artists engaging in technological processes compound poetry's already complex foundations, resulting in the need for viewers to be prepared to approach the task of reading in new ways' (2012, p. 12). It is with such views in mind that we approach digital poetry from a social semiotic perspective, which provides for multi-layered analyses of the ways in which written, spoken and visual signs function to communicate. Another layer of analysis will be added to this chapter, given the use of figurative and literary language in these poems; we will be using terms found in literary stylistics, much in the same way readers use these terms to describe the ways linguistic and aesthetic features make meanings in traditionally printed poetry.

Upon completion of this chapter, you will be able to apply key concepts from multimodal analysis to digitally produced poetic texts, along with describing the use of affordances across the subcategories of text montage poetry, animated poetry and hyperpoetry. You will also be able to apply some of the terms found in literary stylistics in order to describe specific features of language.

Analysing multimodal texts

In Chapter 4 we introduced a framework for analysing images found in texts which also used written language. In those texts, the images tended to draw from the same meanings as the words represented in the texts, and in some cases they provided additional context, which could include social ideologies. Applying Kress and van Leeuwen's (2006) framework, we described features of images as representations which follow **presentational** and **conceptual patterns**. Presentational patterns refer to the participants as belonging to a narrative; as mentioned in Chapter 4, these visual narratives express the ideational meaning of language and can be examined within **transitivity** analysis using the terms *participants*, *processes* and *circumstances*. Conceptual patterns refer to participants' generalised characteristics, such as class, age and social significance. Here we will explore these frameworks further as they are integral to linguistic analysis of digital poetry.

A key concept in understanding the ideational function of visual texts can be found in the understanding of vectors. These are the lines the eyes follow between elements of an image, suggesting a relationship or process occurring. For example, in Figure 5.1, taken from the animated poem 'How my brain betrays me' (by poet Miriam Barr and visual artist Kate Barton), which will be discussed in more detail in the fourth section, the arrow-like lines point in the direction of the hand holding open a very small book. These lines serve as vectors to what is central in this image; this incidentally corresponds to the spoken words about 'reading tea leaves'. The hand can also be seen as a vector, which appears to be pointing to the cup, or at least leading our eyes in that direction.

In these ways, vectors are also involved when creating narratives in images as they suggest that the participants are doing something and often make the link between participant and goal. More specifically, we begin with the main descriptive concepts which we will draw from

Figure 5.1 Screen image from 'How my brain betrays me'
Source: Barr, M and Barton, K (2008) 'How My Brain Betrays Me,'
http://www.youtube.com/watch?v=xUfMgbknvnQ

in this chapter, namely, those of *actor, goal, process* and *circumstance*. The actor is a participant from which a vector emanates; in transitivity analysis, this can also be described as the sensor, sayer, and so on, depending on the type of process. In Figure 5.1 the hand could be described as the main actor, involved in the processes of holding and pointing. In the background, birds are flying, and hence birds would be another actor. The goals are passive participants to which the vectors lead; for example, the lines are pointing to the hand (the goal), and the hand is holding the book (the goal). The process accounts for what is represented in language by verbs and can therefore refer to actions, reactions and relational concepts (such as in the verb 'to be'). In Figure 5.1 other processes include flying, for which there is no obvious goal, and pointing, where the goal appears to be the centre of the image with the hand. The circumstance is a rather broad category, which in language is often described by adverbials, such as prepositional phrases. In this case, the circumstances might be 'at a table' or 'from the sky'.

According to Kress and Van Leeuwen, vectors also include the contrast between foreground and background; in other words, which elements of an image are presented more prominently. In Figure 5.1

the hand and book are foregrounded, thus making them the key focus at that stage of the poem. In addition, vectors can be represented in other ways, such as by a tree diagram or a graph, where relationships between elements are suggested by various lines; this will be useful to consider when we examine navigational maps as part of the ideational meaning in some hyperlinked poetry and fiction.

When looking at images, the interpersonal meaning involves elements representing social relations between the producer, the viewer and the object (which combined could be described as the tenor), along with the **modality** suggested by the image. In language, modality relates to the attitude of the speaker or writer to the subject of communication. Visually, modality is expressed in the way that images or elements of images are presented as more real or true. For example, drawn sketches may be seen as having low modality, that is, they are not true representations; photographs, however, are seen as having high modality. In this instance, the sketch of the hand and teacup is therefore perhaps best described as having medium modality. In a similar manner, different colours can be said to have different semiotic meanings because of their uses in different social contexts. For example, traditionally in Western culture black is a symbol of death and dying; in some Eastern cultures, however, white serves this purpose. Bearing in mind that the meanings ascribed to colours are variable and dependent on culture, we can also examine the use of colours and shades as representative of modality. For instance, colour saturation can be seen on a scale of modality, where the absence of colour (i.e., black and white) suggests the lowest modality. On the other hand, colour saturation, that is, too much colour, might suggest a low-medium modality, whilst the highest modality is indicated by a distribution of colour reflecting that found in the real world. The black, grey and white of Figure 5.1 reflect its low modality, as do the sketch drawings. When reading images found in digital poetry, these different levels of modality communicate not only meanings, but also aesthetic and emotive qualities and sensations.

The interpersonal function of language includes the tenor of communication. In visual images this is described in terms of the image act (i.e., the way the image is intended to do something to the viewer) and the gaze; for example, a person looking straight at the viewer of the image could be seen as making a demand. Of course, image acts and gazes can also be features between the participants within an image, whereby the viewer is playing the role of an observer. Here we can also consider the relative size of the participants in an image, for example, a close shot might imply an intimate/personal relationship, whereas a long shot could suggest an impersonal relationship with the viewer. In Figure 5.1, the distance of the image of the hand and teacup is somewhere between medium and close up, which suggests some level of intimacy with the viewer.

As we have said in previous chapters, the textual meaning relates to the coherence and cohesion of a text. Here we shift our attention to the way different compositional arrangements of words and images allow for different meanings to emerge; this includes the way images communicate meanings through shapes. For example, squares and rectangles dominate our urban world, and their appearance outside of urban landscapes could still carry those associations with them. Circles are said to suggest something complete unto itself. We will see examples of the use of shapes later in this chapter.

To illustrate the textual meaning of an image we return to Figure 5.1, where the cohesion of elements and the coherence of the piece are somewhat limited. There appear to be two distinct images within the frame. The hand at the table with the teacup forms the main image, and is set indoors. The birds flying around a rock formation in the background, as a drawing on the wall, could be seen as a secondary image and is set outdoors. The diversity of these images serves as an apt example of how sociocultural understandings can be seen as resources which viewers and readers draw from in interpreting such texts. As these two images are brought together in this one screen image, the reader creates meanings to allow these images to co-exist in one image. We will see in the analysis below (Animated poetry) how these two images are also brought together through the mode of spoken language; the voiceover reciting the poem links the various images, along with the arrow-like lines coming across the screen.

Thus, while we have isolated images here in order to illustrate how SFL can be applied to images as well as to words, analysing these meanings of language in multimodal texts ideally involves consideration of all of the modes. For this reason, we will also take into consideration sounds, such as spoken language and music, although we are obviously constrained by the printed page.

> **Activity**
>
> Watch Eduardo Kac's 'Tesao' (digital poem) (http://www.youtube.com/watch?v=TpvkNVK0_BY). It refers to itself as a poem, yet it has no words. Given our discussion of meanings assigned to shapes and colours above, what meanings do you find in this work?

Text montage poetry

Before digital technologies came into everyday life, the concept of montage poetry referred to individual poems with texts brought together from different authors or sources. Today, the term 'text montage' has a range of meanings, including the recreation of photographic images by using words of different colours and shades to form shapes across a screen. By narrowing our definition to digital poetry presented in a text montage, we are referring to a type of digital poetry which contains a mixture of static images and poetic text. In these cases, words are integrated into images and themselves serve as shapes which are part of the visual design (Dillon, 2005). We begin with an example of text montage poetry by Stef Zelynskyj entitled 'The Shadow' (Figure 5.2), which is here reproduced in black and white.

This text montage poem has been created by using an existing poem, 'The Shadow', which was written by Ben Jonson (1573–1637). The word *Shadow*, appearing as the title of the poem, is foregrounded, as is the shadowy, headless figure repeated in three places. Only a few patches of green and blue appear for the grass and sky; otherwise this is lacking in colour. The written text is repeated in five places, yet due to its fragmentation it remains unreadable except for the odd word or phrase, such as 'she denies you' and the pronouns *she* and *her*. These words suggest a love poem, but placed with these images, readers might think that the field of this has to do with a lover who has died and is now only a shadow in the poet's memory. Though it should be noted that the figure is walking towards the viewer or reader, this does not give us a clear sense of a goal, or suggest a strong narrative. While the image as a whole is presented at a medium distance, neither a close-up nor a long-distance shot, the lack of a face yields an impersonal tenor. Therefore, it could be argued that, though

Figure 5.2 'The Shadow' by Stef Zelynskyj
Source: http://courses.washington.edu/hypertxt/cgi-bin/book/wordsinimages/unstabelerels.html#textmon

limited, the somewhat formal register of the words which appear in the fragments of texts also helps to create this distance between writer and reader.

The poem, however, can be read differently as a text montage poem than if it were just text on its own. Consider now the text from 'The Shadow' taken from Ben Jonson's (1573–1637) poem below:

> Follow a shaddow, it still flies you;
> Seeme to flye it, it will pursue:
> So court a mistris, shee denyes you;
> Let her alone, shee will court you.
> Say, are not women truely, then,
> Stil'd but the shaddowes of us men?
> At morne, and even, shades are longest;
> At noone, they are or short, or none:
> So men at weakest, they are strongest,
> But grant us perfect, they're not knowne.
> Say, are not women truely, then
> Stil'd but the shaddowes of us men?

Comparing a woman to a shadow which you cannot catch and yet follows you has a subtle irony to it, which makes this a humorous poem. This is quite a contrast to the tenor created by the image of the poem. Moreover, this light-hearted tenor is also manifested in the short lines and rhyming couplets. The field of the poem involves the relationships between men and women, yet there is only one solitary figure in the montage, though it is repeated a few times, and it is unclear whether the figure is male or female. In the poem, there is no reference to bare trees, sky or grass, all of which appear in the images. The poem itself also conveys mini-narratives about courtship, with the participants doing considerably more than the shadowy figure does in the images.

More importantly, in terms of our analysis, there is a lack of cohesion between the written text and the visual images; as we have said, at first the images appear sombre, which stands in contrast to the poem. Noting the incongruity between image and original poem, Dillon (2005) in his analysis of this text montage, describes the poem on its own thus: '[T]his little misogynistic conceit, so typical of its period, seems unspeakable and not at all funny today' (p. 6). Perhaps it is the modern interpretation of this poem as not being funny which makes meaning when set in this text montage. Since this piece has, after all, been created by a contemporary writer-artist, a reader might be better able to link the serious images to the seriousness of a modern interpretation; comparing women to shadows connotes that women are sinister, especially during a courtship. Other interpretations of this montage might draw more from the intertextual reference to the Jonson poem, placing the images into the context and meanings associated with the original text.

With Web 2.0 technologies, there is now more online about how internet users can create their own text montage poetry (and images) than there are poems by professional writers for analysis.

Activity

Consider these two text montage poems in terms of their textual meaning: Sandy Young's 'can i come along?' (http://courses.washington.edu/hypertxt/cgi-bin/book/wordsinimages/unstablerels.html#textmon) and Rob Collin's 'poetry montage' (http://dreams0in1digital.deviantart.com/art/poem-Read-Poetry-Montage-4567305). To what extent do the words relate to the images? What meanings do you think are being created in these poems?

Hyperpoetry

Hyperpoetry, or hypertext poetry as it is sometimes called, is poetry conveyed by using multiple texts (often called lexia) which are usually joined through hyperlinks to other texts or lexia. In Chapter 7, we will explore hypertext fiction, which uses hyperlinks between lexia to create narratives. However, in this section we look at an example of hyperpoetry which is made up of many texts, but texts which are not linked by recognisable hyperlinks; they are nonetheless retrievable and connected in some form. In other words, readers can read the parts of the poem in a different order and might not be aware of some of the parts at all. Moreover, this example is typical of hyperpoetry in that it is interactive.

'Sydney's Siberia' by Jason Nelson defines itself as being 'infinite click and read', and uses multimodality (the combination of words and images) to great effect. Using a Flash-based infinite zoom platform, this poem is composed of 121 text montages.

The reader is first presented with a picture, accompanied by text, and in some instances child-like scrawls, which can then be clicked on creating a zooming lens effect to reveal a screen of other text montages, which give the appearance of being arranged on one large page. The red box moves around the frame with the movement of the reader's cursor. The reader can then click on their cursor for the image to zoom in.

Biographical information about Jason Nelson tells us that he was based in Newcastle, New South Wales, at the time of composing this digital poem. The title 'Sydney's Siberia' is likely to have its origins in a book review written by John Thompson, in which he describes Botany Bay, Australia, as 'Sydney's Siberia', a place for social outcasts and exiles. This is useful when interpreting the first screen. The only text which every reader will experience is the first frame, the only image which is not contemporary and urban. The image is of an exterior wall, possibly above a door, with a photograph of a man dressed in nineteenth-century clothing; on top of this are the words 'between 1875 and 1877 twelve men and women created the folly history society. their goal was to photograph strangers, build fake histories of important and far reaching deeds and then memorialize them as grand pillars, window adorning guardians civic's future'. This prose introduction to the work suggests that the photographs to follow, as the reader clicks and zooms, will be of strangers in the 1870s. However, the images used throughout are nearly all of buildings and other scenes of a city, with just a few including humans, and these are often in the background, or appear only in shadow form. This juxtaposition of past and present can yield many interpretations, such as the idea that the country's past is ever-present. Clearly, the point of cohesion between this first screen and the rest of the poem is the use of photographs of strangers to memorialise them and build histories; the idea of 'fake histories' could lead the reader of the poem to a belief that references to people and buildings are all fictional.

After a couple of clicks from the image in the first screen, the screen appeared as follows (Figure 5.3):

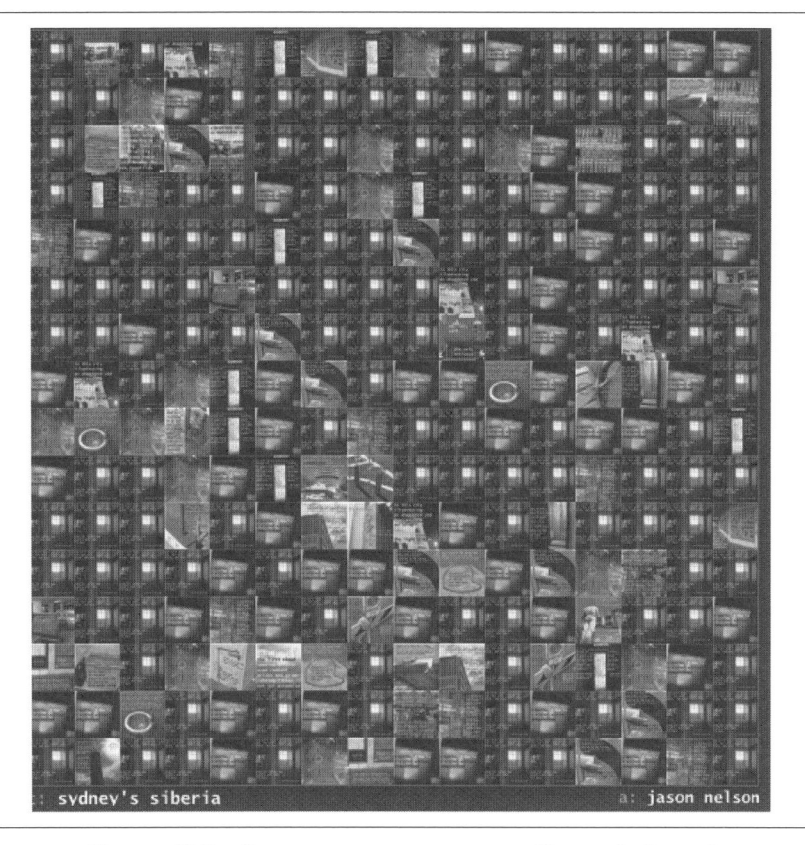

FIGURE 5.3 SECOND SCREEN IMAGE FROM 'SYDNEY'S SIBERIA'
Source: Nelson, J. (2010) 'Sydney's Siberia,' http://www.secrettechnology.com/sydney/sibera.html

86 DIGITAL TEXTUALITY

Clicking a couple more times leads back to a single image frame as in Figure 5.4.

The words on this screen describe the image, with the drawings over the image providing vectors. These vectors emphasise the written text by pointing out the 'light lit bars' and a shadowy figure in the background; this figure is linked to the words 'one third a poet aside'. The written text is arranged as lines typical of the poetry genre as opposed to grammatical sentences. The line 'one third a poet aside' is grammatically deviant in that the reference of 'aside' is not clear; in other words, does it refer to another 'cure for reflecting traffic and light lit bars' or does it stand alone? The narrative suggested by the image is of a person looking out of the window at the traffic and

Figure 5.4 Screen image from 'Sydney's Siberia'
Source: Nelson, J. (2010) 'Sydney's Siberia,' http://www.secrettechnology.com/sydney/sibera.html

parked cars. In Hallidayan terms, the 'still room' in the written text also presents a narrative as being the object of a relational process found in the word 'was'; however, in the image the 'still room' might be described as belonging to the circumstance, the place in which the action occurred.

The reader can continue to follow this path of clicking and reading forever as the images continue to be recycled. This text again promotes reader participation, as they choose their own path through the text.

The cohesion of this work as a whole is more difficult to grapple with and depends on how long readers spend viewing and reading the various texts. While the city scenes across the texts repeat images and urban shapes, there is less cohesion between the written texts. To illustrate this, consider the two written texts extracted from the poem in Figure 5.4 and how they might relate to these texts taken from other screens of this poem:

> Text 1
> torque is a twisting
> force and hinges
> a door's width halved
> are only meant
> for dominant opening,
> acts those so frantic
> to breech is to need
>
> Text 2
> the condition known
> as headarmlessness inflicts
> fancy party dress
> with ghostly precision

Text 1 appears over a metal door in the side of a brick structure, such as an apartment block; so, these words clearly cohere with the images, but they seem less related to the nonsensical verse in Text 2. This second text appears over a photo of a dress-shop window, where the mannequins have no heads or arms; hence there is some cohesion between the modes of words and image.

So what we could say about this poem is that, with the exception of the first image, images cohere across the poem. Within individual frames the text and image cohere. Yet, texts across the poem do not always cohere with one another or appear to be part of the same poem.

88   DIGITAL TEXTUALITY

> **Activity**
>
> Read and view the hyperpoem 'Uncle Roger' by J. Malloy (http://www.well. com/user/jmalloy/uncleroger/partytop.html). Consider these questions: (1) How does the poem use the affordances of the website and digital technology? (2) To what extent can social semiotics and literary stylistics be applied to an analysis of the text?

Animated poetry

Unlike traditional print formats, the affordances of the digital medium allow for the creation of hyperpoetry, as discussed in the last section, and animated poetry, which we will look at here. Given that we are limited by the affordances of the printed pages of this textbook, we need to first consider some of what we are missing, namely the sense of movement. The movements of words and images help to produce meanings for readers of animated digital poetry. For example, smooth, flowing movements of objects suggest different associative meanings than jerky, uneven movements, which for many people imply images made with a hand-held camera. The velocity of moving images can be used in a variety of ways to add meaning to texts; for example, quickly moving images can suggest urgencies or anxiety. Moreover, the changing and contrast of the speed of images, controlled by the creators of these works, might give the impression of **foregrounding** images in order to give them significance. With these points in mind, here we will look at two animated poems: the interactive poem 'Seattle Drift' by Jim Andrews and 'How my brain betrays me' by Miriam Barr and visual artist Kate Barton.

'Seattle Drift' features a piece of text which reads and looks like something which could be found in a book. It appears on a black screen with white letters.

SEATTLE DRIFT
I'm a bad text.
I used to be a poem
but drifted from the scene.
Do me.
I just want you to do me.

If readers choose to become an active participant in the work, they can select the options at the top of the screen in red letters to 'Do the Text', 'Stop the Text' and 'Discipline the Text'. When the reader chooses to 'Do' the text, the letters move around the screen before shuffling off the edges. In other words, the text literally drifts as the words in the poem suggest. At any point while the letters are moving to the edges of the screen, the reader can choose to 'Stop', which stops the letters and holds them in their position, as if suspended on the page. The reader can also choose to 'Discipline' the text, which makes the letters quickly return to their original state, as if being scolded. Without the affordances of digital animation, the text still appears as a poem and has some of the linguistic qualities of poetry, such as the personification of the text and the **polysemy** in the word 'drift' – it could refer to physical or emotional moving away from someone of something, and could also be a playful reference to the Formula Drift Seattle car races. Interpreting this poem without its animation and interactive features does, however, leave an unclear reading of the invitation to 'do me'.

The animation of the text unites the field provided by the image with that of the words. It is a poem about drifting and controlling the text. The vectors in the moving image suggest a mini-narrative of drifting away. The tenor in this brief poem is informal and suggestive of a relationship between reader and text which might be interpreted as similar to parent and child or sadistically between two lovers, which in a sense reverses the power relationship between reader and poem, as the poem gives the orders (in the command 'Do me') and the reader follows by clicking on the words on the screen.

Looking to the textual meaning of 'Seattle Drift', the changing arrangement of the text clearly gives it coherence. Cohesion can be found in the repetition of some words across the instruction text and the poetic text. In addition, the semantic associations between 'bad poem' and 'discipline' also provide cohesive links between poem and instructions.

'How my brain betrays me' is an animated digital poem, using spoken and written modes as well as images. It can be viewed as a video clip on YouTube and lasts 2 minutes, 43 seconds. Unlike 'Seattle Drift', in 'How my brain betrays me' there is no physical interaction between text and reader, aside from the possibility of controlling the animation by pausing, rewinding and stopping. The words of this poem are spoken throughout, with some of the words also appearing on the screen; these written words then fade as the images change. For ease of analysis, the entire poem is printed below, with the words which also appear in the written mode being set in boldface. The line breaks have been provided by the poet, which for the most part reflect the pauses in the speaker's voice on the video clip.

How my brain betrays me

1   This is not a motor tic
        it is a brain tic
      a **twisted itch**
        every texture is bristled
5   like hook-fingered grass seed
   The marmite smear on the bench stares defiantly
        the tap caught in ceaseless drip rhythm
        soundtracks through a sleep-seeking
        exercise in futility
10 In the morning one step will not follow the next
        my breathing creaks
        I cannot find my mind – didn't lose it
        just put it somewhere safe, out of the way
   Later the road to the water is paved with furry animals split open their
15 insides yelping out
        Murray brakes for seagulls and pigeons though and a little light
        switches on
   There is a glow reflection effect of river ripples projecting onto muddy
   bank
20   standing waist-deep in the water bubbles of something stagnate
        floating by
   Something sharp, anonymous finds my foot in the long grass
        back home I squeeze pus from the wound
        take a shower
25   **love** and then **argue** with my boyfriend
        yelp open apart like the animals on the highway
        and stitch myself back together while I wait for sleep again
   There was a time on the mountain though when I was just a puriri pip
   in my father's fingers
30   waiting to be planted
   Can your tealeaf reading still see this in me?
        I have coffee-stained teeth now, tobacco shackled lungs, nicotine
        fingers, wino spider veins and **splintered synapses**
   But I have kept the pip, the kernel, the seed.

This poem can be interpreted as a reflection on the diversity and complexity of the thought processes which run through our brains and the poet's awareness of her own ageing and impending death. Looking to the language of this piece, we might first notice its phonological features, such as the repetition of words 'tick' (lines 1 and 2) and pip (lines 25–29). Phonological **parallelism** can be found in several lines containing alliteration; for example, the sibilance in line 8, where the /s/ is repeated in 'ceaseless', 'soundtracks' and 'sleep-seeking exercise'. Another salient phonological feature is the rhythm and metre of the poem; like most poetry written in English, this is mostly in iambic meter. One variation to this can be found in line 2, where the single syllable words break the iambic rhythm and create a more strained rhythm; given the importance of line 2 to the overall theme of the poem, this break in rhythm lends itself to the meaning of the work. When considering the semantic level of this poem, we can identify semantic fields to do with animals, nature, birth and illness. Semantic deviation can be found in the metaphors, such as in lines 6 (with the personification of marmite) and 12 (with the concrete qualities given to the mind). At a grammatical level, this poem contains little deviation from the grammatical norms of English. One of the few examples can be found in line 8, with the use of 'soundtracks' as a verb. This, along with the phonological and semantic features which are mentioned, help us to see that this work has what Jakobson (1960) referred to as a poetic function, that is, it focuses on the linguistic qualities of the text for their own sake. In this multimodal text, this might also be seen in the way that some words are foregrounded by being written as well as spoken (highlighted in bold in the poem).

The interaction between spoken word and visual images foregrounds some of the concepts and in doing so shapes their possible interpretations. For instance, line 14 features spoken with the word *road*, and when it is spoken a dashed line appears across the screen, which leads to the next image. Throughout the poem, images appear and fade with the camera lens moving from left to right. In this way the position of images and the use of vectors, such as the dashed line, give the suggestion of a journey happening.

When looking to the tenor of the poem as revealed through the images, we noted earlier that this poem tended to use black and white, which could be seen as low modality and unrealistic. The drawing in

Figure 5.1 taken from this poem also exhibits low modality, but lower than this still are some of the other images in this poem; the animals are simple, childlike drawings with no detail to them (Figure 5.5).

In this example screen, the background remains white, but the line drawings and ink-like splashes are all in red in the original. The colour red appears in three places in the poem; first as in Figure 5.5 with lines 14–15, and 22 when the animals are mentioned again. Red appears to connote lust and anger, as well as danger and destruction. This is shown when the words 'love' and 'argue' are written in black font on red splats in line 22. The colour brown appears briefly in tandem with line 16, as the colour of waves and mud, while green appears briefly for the grass in line 19. Perhaps most interesting is the use of yellow, which suddenly fills in the colour of a seagull in line 15 and then concludes the poem as the colour of the kernel. Yellow seems to connote some sort of hope, as the yellow kernel at the very end of the poem leaves the audience with some sense of hope and not so much sorrow. It could be said that in this digital poem, the use of colours are foregrounded.

We can also see from Figure 5.5 that the interpersonal meaning is realised in the sizing of images in this frame and how they relate to the viewer. This could be described as a medium-distance shot, which

FIGURE 5.5 SCREEN IMAGE FROM 'HOW MY BRAIN BETRAYS ME'
Source: Barr, M and Barton, K (2008) 'How My Brain Betrays Me,'
http://www.youtube.com/watch?v=xUfMgbknvnQ

is neither personal nor remote. Most of the animation is at eye level, which gives the reader equality with the elements in the images, and the poem finishes with a high-angle distance shot, which gives a sense of leaving the world created by the poem.

The shapes which are seen the most in 'How my brain betrays me' are geometrical shapes, mainly squares and triangles. A collection of squares which are placed diagonally and scattered across the screen are seen twice in the poem. These are shapes which tend to dominate an urban world, and suggest order and uniformity in their repetition; and in this case are seen in the more melancholic parts of the poem, as in lines 10–14.

As we can see from this analysis of the poem, meanings are created within and across the modes of spoken and written language and the visual language of image and colour.

Bringing together the three modes used in this poem, cohesion occurs both linguistically and visually. As we pointed out earlier, the repetition of words and identifiable semantic fields exist and these also contribute to the cohesion and coherence of the piece. The images, which might at first glance appear unrelated, link together under similar themes to the semantic fields of animals, nature, birth and illness.

Activity

Watch and listen to 'Solitude' by Ella Wheeler Wilcox (from the poem written in 1883) (http://www.youtube.com/watch?v=KviB-Y4frHw). How does it compare with 'How my brain betrays me', discussed in this chapter, in terms of interpersonal and textual meanings and the ways meaning is created multimodally? You might wish to consider the use of shapes and colours and their relationship to the written words.

Conclusions

In this chapter we have focused on poetry which clearly uses the affordances of digital technology and the conventions of the internet. But this in not to say that other forms of poetry are not widespread on the internet. Poems continue to be published online in forms similar to printed texts – in other words, written on a screen instead of on a printed page. While the readers are free to read the poems and do nothing more, they often have the option of leaving comments or sharing the hyperlinked poetry page through a number of SNSs; this is especially the case for online publications of contemporary poetry. The internet has also been a place for disseminating audio and video clips of poems being read and performed. While the production technology of recording poems in these ways has existed for a long time, the means of dissemination are different, and they include the ability to search poems by author, title and lines of texts.

From the works we have experienced here (and in the activities below), we can observe discernible differences between digital poetry and poetry found in printed matter. The reader of digital poetry is reading multimodally. To describe such reading critically, linguists have developed frameworks from semiotics in order to approach visual images in their own right as creating meaning, as well as their interaction with and relation to the written and spoken word. But this is not to imply that such approaches render these poetic works more successful as communication or make them less complex in their meanings. Funkhouser (2012) summarises this point by saying, 'Poetry, for most, already represents an artistic aberration – something moving away from conventional diction and presenting perceptual challenges; digital poetry's inflation of this, through mediated expansion, may very well create too large a separation from norms […]' (p. 24).

We conclude this chapter with a quote from poet and scholar Loss Pequeno Glazier, who makes this apt comment on the influence of digital poetry:

> […] poets are making poetry with the same focus on method, visual dynamics and materiality; what has expanded are the materials with which one can work. Such materials not only make possible multiple forms of writing, but also, in the digital medium, contributed to a re-definition of writing itself. (2008, p. 1)

Sample project

> Visit this link to read/experience 8 'string poems' by Dan Weber: http://www.vispo.com/guests/DanWaber/. Apply your own SFL and multimodal analysis of these animated poems as individual pieces or as a collection of works and in doing so consider how concepts such as metaphor and personification are manifested.

Further reading

Articles on digital poetry occasionally appear in linguistics journals, such as *Language and Literature* (available at: http://lal.sagepub.com/) and *The Journal of Literary Semantics* (available at: http://www.degruyter.com/view/j/jlse)

Amerika, M. (2007) *Meta/data: A Digital Poetics*. Cambridge, MA: MIT Press.

Part scholarly history and part memoir, with some fiction thrown in, this book serves as an enjoyable introduction to digital poetics and digital art. Chapters on internet writing are particularly worthwhile for students of linguistics and digital media.

Funkhouser, C.T. (2012) *New Directions in Digital Poetry: 1*. London: Continuum.

This book undertakes close readings of 24 digital poems, posing questions of current theoretical approaches and our understanding of emerging genres.

Kac, E. (2007) (ed.) *Media Poetics: An International Anthology*. Bristol: Intellect.

This scholarly collection of articles can be rather technical at times, but covers a large range of platforms and ways of producing digital poetry. Discussions on theories and approaches might be seen as an extension of the social semiotics used in this chapter.

Kress, G. and van Leeuwen, T. (2006) *Reading Images: The Grammar of Visual Design*. Abingdon: Routledge.

This has become a seminal work in the analysis of images. It draws from theories in social semiotics, in particular Halliday's SFL as a framework for analysing images, as we have done in this chapter.

Schäfer, J. and Gendolla, P. (eds) (2010) *Beyond the Screen: Transformations of Literary Structures, Interfaces and Genres*. Germany: Transcript Verlag.

This scholarly collection of articles includes several which specifically address digital poetry, looking at challenges to literary theory and aesthetics.

Short, M. (1996) *Exploring the Language of Poems, Plays and Prose*. Harlow: Pearson Education.

This classic textbook in literary stylistics has four chapters about the language of poetry. Though not based on Halliday's SFL, tenor is included. Detailed analysis of foregrounding and deviation with examples and exercises make this a useful book.

Websites used in this chapter

Andrews, J. 'Seattle Drift', http://www.vispo.com/animisms/SeattleDrift.html#

Barr, M. and Barton, K. (2008) 'How My Brain Betrays Me', http://www.youtube.com/watch?v=xUfMgbknvnQ

Nelson, J. (2010) 'Sydney's Siberia', http://www.secrettechnology.com/sydney/sibera.html

Zelynskyj, S. (no date) 'The Shadow', http://courses.washington.edu/hypertxt/cgi-bin/book/wordsinimages/unstablerels.html#textmon

6 Fiction and Collaboration Online

Introduction

This chapter looks at collaborative writing practices online which involve the production of fictional texts. Unlike the collaborative writing involved in online learning, such as Wikipedia, fictional texts involve different platforms and ways of using the internet. As these are works of fiction, the resulting texts also demand different forms of analysis, alongside the social semiotic approaches used throughout this book. Here we will also adopt Text World Theory (TWT) to analyse the fictional narratives produced. Using these approaches in tandem for analysing fiction will continue in Chapter 7, where we examine fiction which is single-authored and produced in online and offline computer-generated platforms. In this chapter, we will examine one work led by a professional and award-winning writer, Kate Pullinger, and another collaborative work by aspiring writers.

Upon completion of this chapter, you will be able to describe how online writing affords a variety of collaborative communication practices. In addition, you will be able to analyse collaborative fiction as communication using SFL and apply concepts from TWT for online fiction.

By way of introduction to the topic of collaborative fiction writing and the affordances used by participants, here we will briefly consider some of the other attempts and ways in which online interaction has worked to produce, or not produce in some cases, enjoyable fiction. One of the first collaborative novels online was *A Million Penguins*, an experimental wikinovel launched by Penguin Books in collaboration with De Montfort University in 2007. While some established and aspiring writers contributed attempts at a novel on the site, others used the international reach afforded by the internet as a platform for advertising and expressing personal beliefs on contentious subjects. In April 2008, the Institute of Creative Technologies of De Montfort University published *A Million Penguins Research Report*, which concluded:

> What today appears not to be a novel as we know it may in time come to be seen as one, just as work once judged not to be poetry is often later brought into the critical fold. But for the moment at least the answer to whether or not a community can write a novel appears to be 'not like this'. Our research has shown that 'A Million Penguins' is something other than a novel [...]

Counter to this, Jinjiang, a collaborative writing site in Chinese, successfully produces time-travel romance fiction. The format of the main text pages of Jinjiang exploits the affordances of a split-screen creation of texts: one for authors and the other for readers. Within each screen or window of texts are columns for authors' recommendations, readers' comments and rankings of each story instalment. The commentary spaces are also for those who oversee the website, called Webmasters, to ensure users follow the guidelines and to encourage continued use with feedback on the contributions. The roles of author, contributing readers and Webmaster appear somewhat fluid as lively discussions build about the fictional works, crossing the boundaries of these roles. While the contributions are by-and-large written text, drawings and illustrations can also be found. The site continues to grow with more subgenres of time-travel romance fiction, and some of the resulting works have been published as paper books. According to Feng (2012), 'reader and author behaviour generated by these romances challenges traditional theories about the process of fiction writing and the demarcation between author and reader' (p. 62). Broadly, this holds true for all of the works examined in this chapter, as we will see in the discussions below.

Another example of digital fictional texts created collaboratively can be found in examples of Twitter Fiction. This elaborate network of fiction, which can be found by searching on Twitter using #twitterfiction, includes standalone fiction of 140 characters and serialised fiction by one author, as well as collaborative fiction. Collaborative works tend to share an additional hashtag in order to allow readers and contributors to follow the appropriate series of tweets. Given the speed with which tweets can be produced, however, collaborations are sometimes treated more as games, asking participants to 'play along' and see how quickly they can think of and write tweets which continue the storylines.

Text World Theory

TWT is going to be utilised in this chapter and in Chapter 7 for the analysis of narrative fiction in a collaborative setting; as it will be applied in conjunction with SFL and semiotic approaches to visual texts, here we introduce the basic principles behind this. Gavins (2007) describes TWT as 'a model of human language processing which is based on the notions of mental representations found in Cognitive Psychology and which shares the experimental principles of Cognitive Linguistics' (p. 8). When it comes to the analysis of literature, cognitive approaches are more focused on the reader's experience of the text than the writer's production of the text, which broadly describes the approaches found in literary criticism and literary stylistics. But this is not to say that the production aspect of a text is outside of a cognitive framework. Gavins (2007) also notes that TWT is a 'discourse framework' which takes into account all participants in a discourse and the contexts in which a text is produced and received. According to TWT, all linguistic communication operates on at least two levels.

The first level of communication in TWT is the **discourse world**, which refers to the conceptual space shared by discourse participants, which for online fiction are writers and readers. This level includes the context of the discourse situation, shared background knowledge of things in the real world along with the text, as it develops among discourse participants. The discourse world 'offers a means of exploring how a range of contextual factors have the potential to impact upon the construction and comprehension of a given discourse' (Gavins, 2007, p. 10). The discourse world is an especially useful notion when analysing collaborative fiction as it allows us to see that communication is a process of negotiation between author and reader, involving both the text of the communication and their personal and cultural background knowledge. In the case of collaborative fiction, incomplete texts or texts written in instalments present us with a developing discourse world.

Of course, the idea of a discourse world can seem too large to grapple with in that it is trying to deal with context, which can include large amounts of shared knowledge. When examining written fictional texts, the discourse world is described as split, as writers and readers are not in the same spatial and temporal locations; this in effect reduces some of the participants' shared conceptual space. Moreover, TWT manages this context with what it calls 'the principle of text-drivenness'. This principle explains that from all of the knowledge and experience held in the minds of participants, it is the *text* being read (or spoken) which determines which elements of knowledge and experience are needed in order to process that text within the discourse at hand. So, for example, readers of the romance time-travel fiction on the Jinjiang website mentioned earlier will draw only from their knowledge of the time periods covered in each story text, and this knowledge is part of the discourse world; readers' knowledge of other time periods would not be included for the sake of analysis, even though such knowledge exists.

The second level of communication is the conceptual space created by the text of the communication itself. Text worlds are further defined as being made up of '**world-building elements**' and '**function-advancing propositions**'. World-building elements account for the sense of time and place and the objects and characters of the text. Function-advancing propositions account for the states, actions and processes which move a story forward. While both world-building elements and function-advancing propositions are constructed within the mental representations of text worlds, there are generic conventions expected by readers which impact upon their understanding and reception of text worlds. In the romance time-travel example, readers are likely to expect the characters to include two lovers, as part of the world-building elements, and their attempts to find each other or remain together, as part of the function-advancing propositions. As we will see in our analyses below, world-building elements and function-advancing propositions can be understood by using Halliday's SFL, specifically the **transitivity** terms of processes and participants. (This use of SFL is also taken up by Gavins, 2007.)

When studying the reception of fiction, it is not unusual to have more than one text world within the text. This is referred to as 'world-switches'. If we think of this in terms of a conversation, we often switch topics within conversations; each topic might be seen as a different text world with its own subjects and issues. Similarly with fiction, each text world might contain its own characters and setting and might embody its own spatial temporal setting, in other words, flashbacks and flashforwards. Another text world within a main text world can be seen in direct speech; where direct speech occurs in past tense narration, there is a time shift from the past to the present and the frame of spatial-temporal reference changes from that of the narrator to that of the characters. In the systematic study of text worlds, the notion of world-switching is particularly insightful in showing the texture and complexity of written texts; this will be illustrated in the two sites examined below.

The relationship between discourse world and text world is one of integration and distinction at the same time. As we have noted, in its construction the text world becomes part of the discourse world – that is, a shared conceptual space – from which further text world elements can be created. Yet, at the same time, the text world remains a different type of world than the discourse world. Werth explains that the discourse world 'is based on perception, backed up by knowledge of the elements perceived' and by contrast the text world is a total construct 'dependent on resources of memory and imagination, rather than direct perception' (1999, p. 17). It is also worth noting that it is this elicitation of 'memory and imagination' in the construction of the text world which involves each reader individually, and as such the meanings of texts are dependent on the individual reader's prior experiences and their frames of reference.

With these relationships between discourse world and text world in mind, we can describe the last of the levels of communication set out by TWT, that of modal worlds. These worlds involve the creation of other conceptual spaces within the text world. Werth (1999) describes these as 'sub-worlds' which are subordinate to the world-building elements and function-advancing propositions of the text world and which define other worlds outside of the parameters of the initial text world. A simple example of a **modal world**, or sub-world, would be a character's daydream, full of wishes and imagined scenarios.

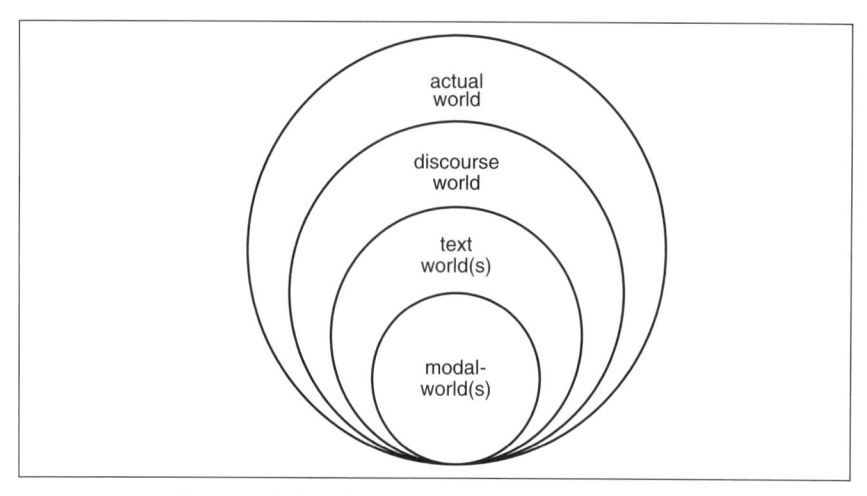

FIGURE 6.1   SUMMARY OF TEXT WORLD THEORY

A more refined definition from Stockwell (2002) describes these worlds as representing 'a variation in texture of the world in focus, without the sense of leaving the current text world' (p. 140). Following current scholarship in TWT, we are describing these worlds in terms of **modality**, namely: (1) boulomaic modal worlds, which represent desires; (2) deontic modal worlds, which relate to obligations; and (3) epistemic modal worlds, which depict the hypothetical worlds, or possible worlds, set out by the narrator or characters. We will explore these modal worlds in the two examples below of online collaborative fiction and in the Chapter 7, which looks at hypertext fiction.

To sum up the levels of communication as described by TWT, we can consider the diagram in Figure 6.1 to show the relationships between these levels of discourse, bearing in mind that these worlds are in constant development. Over-layering these worlds are world-switches. As this chapter is intended to introduce this approach, we have also introduced world-switches; other elements of world production will be added to this in Chapter 7, where we examine hypertext fiction.

Flight Paths

This website refers to itself as a 'networked novel' and to its authors as Kate Pullinger, Chris Joseph and 'participants'. The roles of the participants have changed over the years, and at the time of writing only the original main story by Kate Pullinger, with images by Chris Joseph, remains. The other participants at one time posted readers' suggestions for development of the main work along with video clips which picked up on some aspect of the main story; in addition, there were non-fictional texts, such as autobiographical stories and links and commentaries associated with news stories. A later development included an automated uploading of photos from Flickr, the photo-sharing SNS, in response to tags, such as 'flight paths' and 'Sainsbury's', both of which feature in the main story. For the purposes of our analysis, we will look at a 2012 version of this website, as participants' contributions were viewable at that time (contributions by readers are still being accepted, but only through email). For *Flight Paths*, the main story is told as a **linear** narration, employing mostly written texts, along with related images and music. Some of the images and texts are animated, where the reader cannot control the pace of viewing or reading. This main story is made of six chapters which the reader can access by clicking on the chapter icon on the website's main screen. Most of the story is told with written words across the screen which the reader follows at their own pace by clicking on an icon to move to the next screen. The story is continued and enlarged with readers' contributions displayed at the same website. These include photos, videos and written factual and fictional texts, creating a novel which is multilinear and multi-authored. Here we will first examine the main story of *Flight Paths*, employing a more detailed TWT account to the first few chapters as a way of illustration.

The field of the main story involves the lives of Yacub and Harriet, two strangers who are brought together under unusual circumstances. In summarising the key features of the field, we are also describing aspects of the text world and world-switches to text worlds and modal worlds within it. In Chapters 1 and 2 we have Yacub's story, which makes up one text world within the text of *Flight Paths*. He learns about well-paid jobs in Dubai and goes even though he has been told that the conditions will not be good. He arrives in Dubai and describes the bleak conditions of the many men working at a construction site. Between Chapters 1 and 2 it appears Yacub has returned home, and in Chapter 2 he has decided to return to Dubai, but this time he has been given instructions on how to gain access to a plane bound for Dubai, which is parked on the tarmac; Yacub climbs into a plane through the wheel compartment. Chapter 3 presents the reader with a world-switch into a world where Harriet is the narrator. Throughout this chapter Harriet is driving to Sainsbury's, and her internal dialogue is about all of the food in her house, listing the foods which different members of the family will and will not eat.

The differences between Yacub's world, in Chapters 1 and 2, and Harriet's world, in Chapter 3, are particularly significant to interpreting the story. Drawing from the discourse world, we fill in the context of Yacub's situation, his need to travel overseas as a migrant worker; likewise, Harriet's narration about her family and shopping for them draws from our understanding of modern Western family lifestyles. Table 6.1 illustrates the contrastive text worlds of Yacub's world and Harriet's world as set out in Chapters 1 and 3, by considering the world-building elements, which are summarised, and function-advancing propositions found in the written text portions.

The world-building elements in the text worlds detailing both Yacub's and Harriet's perspectives are expressed using mostly relational processes, as in the sentences 'The plane to Dubai was full of men like me', and 'There is a ton of food in the house'. Such processes tend to identify entities as having certain qualities. Harriet's world contains more world-building elements, such as her descriptions of the pantry and cupboards at home, along with how she identifies herself; this is also expressed with relational processes, as when she says 'I am a good mummy' and 'I am a good wife'.

While the worlds of Yacub and Harriet appear different, there are similarities in some world-building elements, such as family and being in Britain. Readers could make cross-world inference linking these two situations together. We can also see from this table how Yacub is involved in more function-advancing propositions where he is the agent of processes, as he 'went' and 'heard'; in Harriet's world, while she is the agent of 'driving', her family and items of food, such as peas, dominate as agents of processes. Moreover, Yacub's actions include more sensory and mental processes as he describes his new experiences. Harriet's experiences are encapsulated more in deontic modal worlds around her obligations to others.

Recognising the tenors of discourses involved in the two narrations, we can also see the different worlds inhabited by these two characters through differences in their registers of speech found in their first-person narrations. Yacub's style of speech follows a matter-of-fact

TABLE 6.1   Summary of world-building elements in Chapters 1 and 3 of *Flight Paths*

World-building elements

Text worlds of Chapter 1	*Text worlds of Chapter 3*
Time: present day	Time: present day
Places: a village in the UK and Dubai	Place: Richmond, UK
Characters: Yacub	Characters:
Yacub's family	Harriet's family
A man from the village	
The men working in Dubai	
Other settings:	Other settings:
In a bus	In a car
Worksite in Dubai	Inside Sainsbury's
	Sainsbury's car park
Objects:	Objects:
Money	Food (details of specific foods)
	Pantry
	Cupboard full of food

Function-advancing propositions

Yacub's world	*Harriet's world*
I went to Dubai	(Title: Harriet driving)
I heard I could earn good money	I have to go to the supermarket
The man in my village was injured	The peas have fallen/are rolling
I knew what to suspect	The family expects meals
I liked the look of Dubai	They know that fairies do not replenish the cupboards
We were transported to the camp	

reporting style, which is somewhat formal and suggestive that English is not his first language. Harriet's speech, more informal than Yacub's, articulates a housewife's register by its choice of words and reveals something of her own personality through hyperbole and sarcasm. The two texts below help to demonstrate this.

> Text from Chapter 1 (Yacub):
> The plane to Dubai was full of men like me, all ages, although I was one of the youngest. When we landed we were transported to the camp where we were to live.

Text from Chapter 3 (Harriet):
I have to go to the supermarket today, otherwise my family will starve. Well, not starve exactly. In the event of a war or cataclysm, of some kind, there is enough food in the house to last for – how long?

As this is a multimodal text, the contrasts between Yacub's and Harriet's worlds are also manifested through images and sounds. The text from Chapter 1 appears in Figure 6.2. Typical of this chapter, the images are dark, with black and grey sketches and photographed images over a dark yellow background. Chapter 2 occurs mostly at the airport in the darkness of night. Both of Yacub's chapters are characterised by still images which shift across the screen, some overlapping on to others (Figure 6.2).

An example of text from Harriet's world appears in the image in Figure 6.3.

Most of this chapter depicting Harriet's world is bright white, and unlike the shifting of still images across the screen, these images are more filmic and constantly moving. Often two or three moving images

Figure 6.2 Screen image from Chapter 1 of *Flight Paths*
Source: http://www.flightpaths.net/

of street scenes appear on the same screen. Such images contribute to the meanings found in the world-building elements of the text worlds, but interestingly they do not contain the images of the main characters and, thus, their function-advancing propositions are limited to the narrative of secondary characters and those form part of the setting. For example, the images of the men working at the construction site suggest the proposition of 'men working'. The reader conceptualises the function-advancing propositions of Yacub's and Harriet's worlds for the most part through the written text, as shown in Figure 6.3. The contrasts between these worlds are also exemplified by the music. Yacub's world in Chapter 1 has Eastern-style music, while Harriet's is popular Western-style music. In Chapter 2, single bass notes can be heard, which are similar to suspense-film soundtracks.

The modal worlds in these early chapters emerge from Yacub's desire to earn money, which are classified as belonging to a boulomaic modal world, and with this an epistemic modal world where he imagines the possibility of earning money and later of getting paid. As we noted above, one of Harriet's modal worlds could be characterised as deontic, as she expresses her obligation to feed her family.

Chapter 4 switches back to Yacub's world and begins with him looking for the secret passage to the cargo hold. Once the plane has taken off, he sits on a 'shelf' in the plane, and the scene changes to a split screen with the darkness of Yacub's world on one side and Harriet's world on the other side, with its brightly lit rows of shelves in

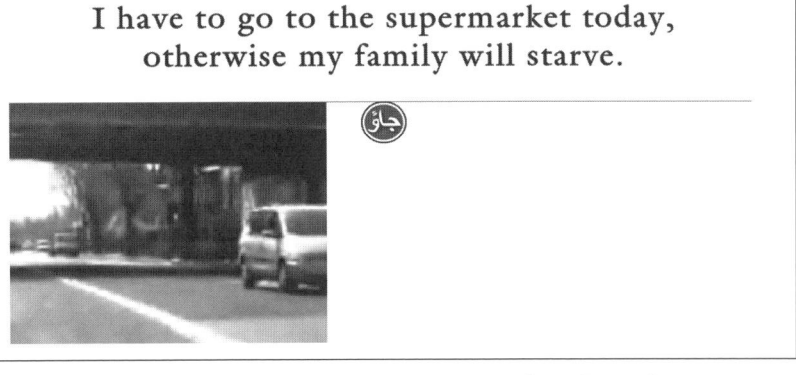

Figure 6.3 Screen image from Chapter 3 of *Flight Paths*
Source: *Flight Paths* by Kate Pullinger, Chris Joseph and 'participants' http://www.flightpaths.net/

the Sainsbury's supermarket. As the split screen continues, the reader experiences the two worlds by going back and forth between them and perhaps for the first time assumes that these worlds are happening within the text world of the story at the same time. Here we can also identify another boulomaic modal world of desires for Yacub, as the space he is in is too small and frightening. Harriet experiences anxiety with her trolley of groceries in a car park, which is comfortably large and busy; this could also be seen as a modal world. At the boot of her car Harriet happens to look up at the clear blue sky. At this point the music stops and the screen shows a moving image of a sky with words where, for the first time, the reader cannot control the pace of words. The image of the sky continues until Yacub, having fallen from the plane, crashes onto the roof of Harriet's car. In this final climatic scene there are no specific images to support the words, aside from the sky; thus, the reader's mental representations fill in the story and emotions as they would if reading a book. This further exemplifies how readers rely on the discourse world and its complexities, as an understanding of this dramatic scene involves bringing together these characters' stories, along with an understanding of what it might be like to fall from a plane and to be the person on the ground watching someone fall from a plane.

In Chapter 5, which was the final chapter of the main story until mid-2012, Harriet waits in silence as the crumpled-up figure on the top of her car comes to life. Yacub sees her trolley of food and comments that he is starving. As her car is wrecked, the two of them go off together in a taxi. This final surreal scene has suggested to some readers who have contributed to the website discussion forum that Yacub actually did die and this scene belongs to another world of a dream, which could be his dream or hers. Other contributing readers have posited that both have died and become ghosts. However this is interpreted, it presents a world-switch for readers, who need to conceptualise a world outside of the world of the car park to explain what has happened or is likely to happen next.

Chapter 6 is narrated from Jack's point of view – at first the reader does not know who he is, only that he is a teenage boy. He tells his story as if it were a computer game, even using expressions such as 'start game' for the click icon to continue the story. Readers might at times feel that they are both playing a game and simultaneously reading a story; this serves as a good example of how digital literature uses the affordances of the medium. The computer-game style of communication is part of the tenor of this chapter. As the chapter continues, Jack finds Yacub hiding in the pantry; Yacub explains that the boy's mother thinks he is dead and that she is the only one who can see him. This chapter is particularly interesting in that it presents the reader with Jack's world and with that world switches to direct speech on a couple of occasions; this is the only chapter of *Flight Paths* to have direct speech. The image in Figure 6.4 from Jack's world illustrates this, as well as demonstrating the tenor of this chapter's images through the use of a shadow to represent Yacub.

At the time of this writing this is where the main story of *Flight Paths* ends.

The readers' contributions which appear on the website can each be treated as other text worlds and as such, each has a different field. For example, there is a news story about a man who was a stowaway on a commercial airline flight into Heathrow Airport, taken from the *London Evening Standard*. Like Yacub in the main story, the man hid

FIGURE 6.4 SCREEN IMAGE FROM CHAPTER 6 OF *FLIGHT PATHS*
Source: http://www.flightpaths.net/

in the wheel compartment and jumped from the plane, miraculously surviving with minor injuries. The worlds presented in this story, which includes direct speech, different participants and settings than those of the main *Flight Paths* story, also have a different tenor. In the example text below, we can see a news reporting register:

> A stowaway clung to the undercarriage of a jet during a flight at 25,000 feet before amazing security men by tumbling onto the tarmac when the plane landed at <u>Heathrow</u>.
>
> The <u>Civil Aviation Authority</u> said today he had been 'incredibly lucky' to have survived. He could easily have been crushed by the wheels and also faced temperatures of minus 41C and a lack of oxygen.

As mentioned earlier, other texts on the *Flight Paths* website include Flickr photographs of birds, planes and Sainsbury's supermarket. While the planes and images from the supermarket provide visual images to feed into the text worlds of the main story, the images of birds actually do not. Such images might be seen as a metaphorical extension of the story, one which draws from other elements in the readers' discourse worlds, or as world-switches to other text worlds which co-exist alongside the worlds of Yacub, Harriet and Jack.

Another notable contribution to the *Flight Paths* website has been a personal narrative from an American student suffering panic attacks while living in Istanbul. The text world presented in this contribution might not at first sight appear directly related to the main story of Flight Paths, as the participants, setting, place and objects are so different from the other texts on the website. Yet, what they could be seen to share is the modal sub-worlds of fears and hypothetical worlds associated with being in countries other than one's own.

These different contributions along with the chapter divisions found in the main story could be brought together into a coherent and cohesive whole, and this can be seen if we examine the textual meaning more closely. We have already mentioned aspects of this meaning by noting the arrangements of images and texts in the main story. Textual meaning also points to the use of multimodal cohesive devices. We have direct repetition of words and their images, as noted above, with 'flight paths' being the title of the main story and the words also appearing in readers' contributions. The text also displays cohesion with the use of **synonyms** (or near-synonyms); Chapter 4, where Yacub's and Harriet's worlds come together, is linked by the 'shelf' in the plane and the images of shelves in a supermarket. In this chapter the two separate worlds are demarcated by **hyponyms**, where the reader would recognise that parts of a plane are likely to be part of Yacub's world and the large car park is part of the supermarket belonging to Harriet's world. As we discussed above, by considering world-building elements and function-advancing propositions, the main story presents two contrasting worlds; these oppositions also help the story elements to cohere, as they are ultimately making meaning out of opposition; for example, Harriet's family having too much to eat contrasted with Yacub's hunger.

This analysis has outlined many of the features of this fiction website using SFL and TWT, and has demonstrated how communication in this format can be brought together in meaning-making with multimodal resources.

Activity

Inanimate Alice is another networked novel from Kate Pullinger, though intended for pre-teen readers. Similar to *Flight Paths*, it is based on pre-created episodes which cannot be altered by readers; however, young readers have created their own versions of the story, either filling in the gaps or developing new strands. Visit the *Inanimate Alice* website (http://www.inanimatealice.com/) and view a couple of the episodes, then visit this reader-created episode: http://www.youtube.com/watch?v=94k4TYfNiWY. Consider the extent to which field, tenor and mode compare across these episodes.

Ficly

Ficly is a collaborative fiction-writing website for new and aspiring writers. Unlike *Flight Paths*, these fictional texts are not multimodal and are only in a written mode. Participants post their stories or parts of a story on to the Ficly website, where readers are given the options to write a 'prequel', 'sequel' and/or a comment. In the example we are going to look at, the original story fragment was followed by another fragment by the same author in the form of a sequel. Another author came in to write the next sequel, which was added to by the author of the first two story postings. This type of collaborative writing is sometimes referred to as 'chain stories' (Rettberg, 2011) and reflects the early days of collaborative writing online. Unlike the early chain stories, however, following each posting are comments, which will be considered as part of the constructed text as these comments remain on the website unaltered. The authors of the story postings can, and have in this case, edited their work on the basis of comments.

The first story posting is entitled 'They came to take me away' by Sam Ervine. This is a first-person narration, written in an informal register. The tenor of this text is also characterised by an interior monologue, as the narrator's inner thoughts are represented. This leaves the reader at a distance from the narrator, who refers to unknown characters and situations only through pronouns, such as 'they' and 'it'. Given this withholding of information, for our analysis, at this stage there is little in the way of a discourse world to draw from except that given in the text for the developing text world. While the context of this initial posting might be limited, the text displays coherence and cohesion by staying with the theme of the narrator being taken away by a group of people. To explore these aspects of the textual meaning further, below are the final paragraphs of this first story posting.

> They're going to take me, take me away. I'm leaving soon. Very soon. They want me. I don't want them. I just want them out. Out of here, out of there, out of everywhere.
>
> I can't leave. They're closer, now. Closing in on the final point. The final stretch. The final countdown. The final capture, the last of the last of the last.
>
> They've nearly got me. I can't escape. I can't delay. I have to act. Perhaps, just maybe, possibly, I could slip by.... oh dear! They've got me! I can't leave! I've much to do! They came to take me away!

From this example we can see the repetition of words and ideas through synonyms (such as 'final' and 'last') to create a writing style suggestive of the narrator's inner thoughts. Given this interior monologue, it is no surprise that this stretch of text is rich in modal worlds. A boulomaic modal world of the narrator's strong desire not to be taken away dominates the text. There are also what Gavins refers to as 'negation worlds' created here by the negatives (such as 'can't leave', and 'can't escape').

Deontic worlds occur with the narrator's obligations to him/herself (such as, 'I have to act' and 'I've much to do'). The epistemic world is constructed a great distance from the underdeveloped text-world, and modals pile up on top of each other here: 'Perhaps, maybe, possibly, could'. In fact, there are so many modal worlds that this adds to the sense of disorientation felt by readers. We have no reliable information about what the text-world of this narrator contains. The language of the text keeps us shifting into his/her mental and hypothetical realms.

This story was followed by a few general comments, where readers expressed that they liked the story and were waiting for the next instalment.

The same author added the following text, which the website treated as a 'sequel'. It is entitled 'I Can't Stop Myself', and the story fragment is reprinted in full below:

> They took me away.
> I've left. Gone away. Disappeared. Vanished. I'm no longer where I was, I'm in a new place.
> I'm stuck in a cell. Locked up, pinned down, held back, chained to the wall.
> It's not that different than my past existence, in fact it's much the same. Forced away from the world.
> No one wants to see me anyway. I'm a loser, freak, jerk, just a general pain in the ass. I should just die…
> … I hear noises. Footsteps are pounding. Machinery is banging. The telephone is wailing. A baby is crying. Where could I be?
> I'm lost, stranded, unfamiliar with my surroundings. I'm not sure where I am.
> When they took me away, they took me somewhere new. Somewhere without any of the comforts of home.
> Am I crazy? Nuts? Insane? Deranged? Mad?
> The door is shaking. The door is sliding. The door is opening.
> They're back. They don't want me here.
> I scramble to the corner of the room. They are faster.
> No … no! I won't go!
> They're taking me away again!
> I can't stop myself, they're taking me away again!

As we can see, the tenor is the same as in the first story, with the interior monologue style of writing and with a few additions to what might be shared knowledge between writer and reader. These additions come about through the new world-building elements, including the place being a cell and the narrator's descriptions of himself manifested through relational processes (e.g., 'I'm a loser' and in the questions 'Am I crazy? Nuts?'). Moreover, the text world is growing with function-advancing propositions, expressed through material process, such as the pounding of footsteps and the opening of the door and a sensory process of hearing.

The comments which followed this sequel were similar to those following the first posting. None of these comments suggested any changes to the texts, or where the story might go to next. But a sequel entitled 'Confrontation' was added by another writer, using the name Lone Writer. As we will see in the text below, this sequel adds new text worlds with a world-switch at the onset of the text.

> 'Where have you taken him?' She demanded furiously, the expression almost laughable on her petite face.
> 'Not where we're taking you.' The man sneered at her, the scar just by his mouth twisting.
> 'Let go of me!' She screamed, 'Leave me alone! He's more powerful than you, he'll escape again!'
> The man just laughed at her. 'With the drugs we've given him, he'll be lucky to even know who you are.'
> 'No,' She started to tremble, tears leaking from her eyes. *'He'll remember.'*
> 'Sure he will,' He replied sarcastically, dragging her out into the alley. She kicked and struggled but he was too big for her. He threw her in the back of the van with the others. 'Take care of her boys.'
> The men in the back of the van grabbed her roughly and duct taped her hands, feet and mouth.
> 'Gently,' One of the others said. 'She's just a girl.'
> 'Shaddup, David!' Another yelled. 'You were always a softie. Just do your job and be quiet.'
> The girl glowered at them from her position on the floor.

This story instalment stays within the general field of the original story about a man being taken away and held captive. But the field has been expanded to activity taking place outside the cell where the man is being kept. A new text world has been added with world-building elements of its own with new characters and a new place setting, which is outside of the cell. The new characters include a girl, and most of the function-advancing propositions revolve around her. Perhaps the most significant change to the story is that the tenor has changed significantly to a more formal register and a third-person narrator, altering the interpersonal meaning of the text between writer and reader. With this different perspective, the story has been switched away from the modal sub-world created in the mind of the narrator in the first few instalments. As a piece of communication, these changes work in as much as the story not only stays within the field but retains a sense of coherence and cohesion with reference to the same entities and processes, such as the man having been confined before. More importantly, these changes to the story as a whole signify the identity of another participant-writer in this communication.

The comments to this sequel add to the discourse world of the story in interesting ways. For example, Sam Ervine, the author of the first two texts, makes these comments: 'Good storytelling. This gives me something to talk about, anyway. I was losing interest in this story arc'. This might be seen as a way of allowing readers to accept these additions. Other comments on 'Confrontation' include the following (with ellipses in the original):

> For a split second the sudden change from first to third person was a tad jarring, but then I fell back into the groove. A new perspective is always interesting … and you've opened up new opportunities about our captive original narrator, almost making him sound demonic somehow…

> Your story's a sort of cliche, but I'll forgive that because it seems to advance the plot of a larger story.

These comments follow the acceptance of the changes by the first author, and perhaps encouraged the story to continue. The second comment above about the story being a cliché makes an understandable criticism formed from a discourse world which probably includes generic conventions of thriller/suspense writing. Interestingly, in this online environment, this criticism is never directly addressed. The final sequel was authored by Sam Ervine again, and starts with a world-switch back to his original narrator, again writing in the first person and with an interior monologue style of writing. These changes back to the original instalment could be seen as signifying the identity of the first author as an individual participant in this communication. This sequel is entitled 'I want to remember' and is reproduced below:

> I awoke. I had apparently been sleeping for a long time. My hair is rumpled, my clothes are off.

> I'm sitting naked in a dark room. There are no doors. There aren't any exits. I can't get out.
> My memory seems very unclear. I can't remember much. Stuck, stuck, stuck, stuck, stuck. I'm stuck.
> Who am I? What have I done, where am I from? Why am I here?
> And who do I know?
> There's an image of someone, floating, reaching out to me … it's a female. A female. A beautiful female. I want to remember … I don't want to forget. I want to jar my memory.
> I close my eyes, concentrating. Focusing. Meditating.
> I can see her face. I think. I'm not sure, I'm confused, mentally lost.
> I have to focus on what I know.
> I'm naked, in a room without any doors, and I know a female. I'm naked, in a room without any doors, and I know a female. I'm naked, in a room without any doors, and I know a female. I'm naked, in a room without any doors, and I know a female….

This world-switch includes elements from the added text world from the previous sequel, namely the character of the woman. Integrating this character provides cohesion across the instalments and bridges the two text worlds of the two principle characters. The use of repetition in this part of the text creates an epistemic modal world as the narrator's mind is questioning the reliability of his thoughts and memories. The other author of this collaborative story, Lone Writer, made this comment about this point: 'Really, good. I think I may just have to sequel you again. I especially like how he repeats it to himself so he won't forget'.

Compared with the collaboration involved in *Flight Paths*, this example from Ficly.com reveals more about the process of collaborative writing and how fictional stories can be communicated online. Levels of communication articulated in TWT have helped us to delineate different authors' contributions as well as describe the development of the story.

Activity

The Web Fiction Guide website (http://webfictionguide.com/) is a collection of stories by aspiring writers, where the reader sees reviews and synopses before entering into the webpages to read the stories or story

> instalments. In this way, the site uses the affordances of the internet. Visit the site and analyse other ways the site uses the internet environment, and compare this with the affordances of reading fiction by traditionally printed means.

Conclusions

As with the previous chapter on digital poetry, social semiotics allows us to approach the communicative and multimodal aspects of texts, with particular consideration to their sociocultural contexts. More importantly, in looking at fictional narratives we have applied TWT, as it has been developed by Gavins (2007), to include the notion of world switches. Social semiotics and cognitive stylistics together highlight areas in which these two approaches complement each other in ways useful to the analysis of networked novels and other similar digital fictions.

Other sociocultural and cognitive approaches could be applied to these texts. For instance, concepts from Bakhtin, such as **heteroglossia,** might help to analyse the marked collaborative communication involved in the production of these texts (in particular, the changes noted above in the Ficly.com story which appear to mark a different author voice as well as different character voices). From cognitive approaches, we could consider the notion of mind style (from Semino, 2002) to highlight how readers know a different authorial voice or focalisation in a narrative multimodal text; we have different mind styles presented in both *Flight Paths* and the Ficly.com story brought on by world-switches.

Sample projects

1. In this chapter we have presented partial analyses of two collaborative fiction websites, focusing on texts within each which help to illustrate the layers of communication involved in the production and reception of these texts. Choose one of the two websites and examine other texts or extracts of texts not yet examined in this chapter.

2. Visit this fiction writing wiki: http://fiction.wikia.com/wiki/Fiction. Randomly choose a 'chapter' to read and then read about the edits and comments. Analyse the chapter using SFL and TWT, then consider the changes and comments and which elements of these approaches they effect.

Further reading

Bell, A., Astrid, E. and Rustad, H. (eds) (2013) *Analyzing Digital Fiction*. London: Routledge.

This collection of articles offers analyses based on methodological frameworks and approaches found in stylistics, social semiotics and narratology, among others. Articles include an analysis of Twitter fiction and another which looks at Kate Pullinger's *Flight Paths* from a multimodal perspective, highlighting cross-cultural and aesthetic qualities of the text.

Feng, J. (2012) 'Have Mouse, Will Travel', in Lang, A. (ed.) *From Codex to Hypertext: Reading at the Turn of the 21st Century*. MA: University of Massachusetts Press.

This article provides a thorough analysis of the Jinjang collaborative writing website. It includes the development of the various sub-genres of time-travel romance fiction in China.

Gavins, J. (2007) *Text World Theory: An Introduction*. Edinburgh: Edinburgh University Press.

This highly readable textbook has been central to the approach of TWT used in this chapter and in Chapter 7. It provides examples where TWT is applied to spoken discourse and non-fiction texts, along with literary texts.

Gibbons, A. (2012) *Multimodality, Cognition and Experimental Literature*. London: Routledge.

Bringing together multimodal analysis and cognitive linguistics, this book examines how readers engage with multimodal literature.

Page, R. (2012) *Stories and Social Media: Identities and Interaction*. London: Routledge.

While the focus of this book is narratives in social media, there is one chapter devoted to online collaborative fiction. Here, the analysis focuses on narrative identities in two online collaborations, *One Million Penguins* (mentioned in this chapter) and *Protagonize*.

Werth, P. (1999) *Text Worlds: Representing Conceptual Space in Discourse.* London: Longman.

Published after Werth's death in 1995, this book was edited and compiled from Werth's drafts by the eminent literary stylistician Mick Short. The coverage of world-building elements is particularly useful. But different from Gavins (2007) and the current trends in TWT, Werth's original work did not contain world-switches, but instead treated flashbacks and flashforwards as sub-worlds.

Websites used in this chapter

A Million Penguins. This website is still running, but appears more as a blog or discussion forum than it appears to be aimed at fiction. http://www.amillionpenguins.com/

Jinjiang website, http://www.jjwxc.net. This website is in Chinese, but translation into English is available via Google.

Flight Paths by Kate Pullinger, Chris Joseph and 'participants' http://www.flightpaths.net/.

http://ficly.com/. This is the home page for Ficly.com. To view the works used here, as well as a host of others, one needs to register either independently or through their other accounts, such as Google or Facebook.

7 Hypertext Fiction

Introduction

In this chapter, as with the previous one, we examine fictional texts written and read on digital platforms. While Chapter 6 focused on collaborative fiction and the creation of online fiction through writer–reader interaction, this chapter looks at hypertext fiction: texts which have one writer, but where the act of reading and the text experienced vary significantly from reader to reader. Upon completion of this chapter, you will be able to describe the textual characteristics of hypertext fiction and to analyse these texts by applying elements of social semiotics and TWT.

Following an overview of characteristics of hypertext fiction and approaches to these digital texts, this chapter will consider three texts: the novel *Patchwork Girl* (Jackson, 1995), the novella *Twelve Blue* (Joyce, 1996) and the short story 'Samantha in Winter' (Stephens, 2004). *Patchwork Girl* can be purchased and downloaded online, while *Twelve Blue* and 'Samantha in Winter' are freely available on the internet. As with previous chapters, social semiotics, drawing from SFL and multimodal analysis, is used to describe communicative features of these texts. We will also employ TWT, which was introduced in Chapter 6, for analysing these works as fictional texts. Both of these approaches have emerged in recent years as key frameworks for analysing and appreciating hypertext fictions.

What is hypertext fiction?

Like many of the other text types discussed in this book, hypertext fiction pieces together smaller, often multimodal texts, called nodes or **lexia**, through a series of hyperlinks. Similar to reading some digital poetry, the reader clicks on the hyperlink in order to move from one lexia to another. Like some digital poetry, the reader often has more than one choice of hyperlink within a given lexia, and with each choice, a different lexia appears. In these cases, each lexia contributes to a narrative, and there could be several narratives in one hypertext, entering the storyline at any point; for these reasons, hypertext fictions are often referred to as non-linear or multilinear. With a multitude of link choices, each reader will have his or her own unique experience of the same hypertext.

The term *hypertext* was coined by the computer pioneer and philosopher Theodore H. Nelson in the 1960s to describe 'non-sequential writing – text that branches and allows choices to the reader, best read at an interactive screen' (Nelson, 1981, cited in Landow, 2006, p. 3). This first definition is still true of hypertext fictions today and serves to highlight the main features which make hypertext different from traditionally printed fiction. Whereas hypertext is non-linear or multilinear, printed fiction is more **linear** and naturally capable of linearity with the turning of pages. While this is generally the case, it needs to be said that non-linear storytelling is not unique to digital fiction, as printed works of fiction, such as many contemporary novels, can also play with the notion of linear time. Another relationship between hypertext and printed text worth noting is that 'we depend in a variety of ways on our knowledge of print in order to read and write hypertexts' (Bolter, 2001, p. 45). While many hypertexts include multimodal lexia, hypertext fictions generally involve reading words within sentences and paragraphs, and these texts adhere to many of the conventions of their paper-based counterparts. However, hypertext fictions have at present established few conventions of their own, especially in terms of document design, which bears significantly on the reading experience. As we will see in the three examples discussed in this chapter, the ways in which readers navigate through hypertext fictions and find lexia vary with each text.

The stark differences between hypertext and printed fiction were at the heart of early approaches to hypertext fictions. Indeed, many early approaches to hypertext tended to focus on the enigma of hypertext narratives and the interactivity required by these computer-based texts, giving the reader control of the narrative experience. The idea of the reader being actively involved in the creation of texts and meanings was described in terms of Roland Barthes' distinction between 'readerly' and 'writerly' texts, with the view that printed texts were readerly, being more passive experiences for the reader, and hypertexts were writerly, where the reader's involvement makes the reader a writer as well. Interestingly, the term *lexia* was taken from Barthes (1974). Other approaches in the early days of hypertext claimed that these texts followed postmodernist thinking. These hypertext theorists highlighted reader control in the way that these texts lend themselves to individualised and open-ended interpretations.

More recent studies on hypertext are more multifaceted in describing the complex role of the reader. On the one hand, the reader is empowered by the mechanisms of the hypertext medium to choose lexia. The reader is empowered in these cases where the choices are guided by associations between the hyperlinked word or image and the destination lexia. However, on the other hand, the reader's choice is random with unclear associations between hyperlinks and lexia; the reader is not so much controlling the reading experience as they are reacting to it. With this second wave of approaches, interest in hypertext has come more into the domain of linguists engaged in the study of online communication and the new genres it has created; literary stylisticians in particular have begun to analyse hypertext fictions as literary texts worthy of the type of literary stylistic analysis applied to printed literature.

From these trends in hypertext theory, three main themes have emerged in the examination of hypertext fiction: (1) reader empowerment; (2) non-linearity and multilinearity; and (3) coherence and cohesion. Here we begin by placing these themes into an SFL framework, considering the manifestation of the interpersonal and textual meanings, as these not only encapsulate these themes, but can also be discussed generally across hypertext fictions. When we examine three texts below in detail, we will include the ideational meaning and apply the elements of all of the meanings; namely, the tenor, field and modes involved.

Interpersonal meaning and reader empowerment

Reader empowerment and the extent of interactivity required for reading a given hypertext fiction can be viewed as part of the interpersonal meaning of communication between writer and reader. For example, the title page of *Patchwork Girl* (Figure 7.1) as it appears on the screen illustrates how hypertext fiction uses its interactivity to establish a communicative relationship between writer and reader. The list below the name 'Mary/Shelley & Herself' are each hyperlinked to lexia which contain parts of the story. The reader needs to choose between these and other links, represented in a story map (Figure 7.3), which are revealed by clicking a button in the toolbar at the top of the screen.

In order to consider the extent to which reader empowerment is present, we need to consider whether or not readers' choices are informed choices, or if they are merely clicking the only options available with no indication of where they may lead. In the example of Figure 7.1, we can see by the titles given to different sections, such as 'graveyard', the choice is informed as the reader will likely go to a text about, or set in, a graveyard. As we will see from examining three different hypertexts, linking can vary from instances where hyperlinked words or images lead the reader to a lexia with a clear semantic association, such as in 'graveyard', to those which are completely unrelated; the explicit semantic associations would seem to empower readers, whereas those links which are unrelated might confuse and disorient

FIGURE 7.1 TITLE PAGE OF *PATCHWORK GIRL*
Source: Jackson, S. (1995) *Patchwork Girl*. Watertown, MA: Eastgate Systems

readers. Moreover, while readers often have choices to make as to which link they click, as noted in current hypertext theory, these links and lexia have been written by the author, who still has some control over the paths taken.

Another feature found in many hypertext fictions which reveals the interpersonal meaning of communicating these texts is the use of a second person. The occurrence of *you* in hypertext fiction operates at different levels. At one level it is no different from its appearance in printed texts, as a way of engaging the reader with the world of the text. At another level, hypertext fiction can use the *you* to manoeuvre the reader across the text, addressing readers to make navigational choices, interrupting the building of the narrative or story world. An example of this can be found in the seminal hypertext novel *afternoon, a story* by Michael Joyce, where the first lexia introduces a fragment of the story and asks the reader, 'Do you want to hear about it?'. The reader can respond by clicking on 'yes' or 'no', each time going to a different lexia.

Textual meaning in hypertext fiction

The ideas of linearity, cohesion and coherence are manifested through the textual meanings of hypertext fictions. It is not unusual for a reader to begin a hypertext fiction with a lexia which appears to be in the middle of a story, with, for example, references to unknown characters, sometimes referred to simply by a pronoun. It is also not unusual for hypertext fictions to appear to have many subplots or storylines. Such features have to do with the arrangement of elements within the overall text.

Given the complex linearity of hypertexts, many theorists have asked if they can be said to have beginnings. Landow (2006) explains that while the typical hypertext narrative has a sense of beginning in the middle of the plot structure, most hypertext fictions 'take an essentially cautious approach to the problems of beginnings by offering the reader a lexia labelled something like "start here" that combines the functions of the title page, introduction and opening paragraph' (p. 227). As we will see in the examples below, some hypertexts start with a map or diagram for navigation. This vague sense of a beginning is akin to a table of contents; however, the reader, unlike one viewing a table of contents in a printed book, would not know where the narrative begins.

Similarly, a great deal has been written in hypertext theory about the lack of endings in these fictions; because parts of the story are not being read in a linear order and there are not always enough clues for the reader to know if he or she is reading about the end of the story, identifying an ending can be difficult. Moreover, depending on the reader's experience and interaction with the text, some parts of the story might be missed out altogether, including the ending. Counter to this, Landow offers the idea that 'hypertext fictions always end because readings always end, but they can end in fatigue or a sense of satisfying closure' (Landow, 2006, p. 229).

Further examination of the typical textual meanings of hypertext fictions highlights the ways these texts attempt to have coherence and cohesion. As coherence has to do with the way a text makes sense and the extent to which it is well formed, linguistic research examining coherence in hypertext fiction has considered, among other things, the role of hyperlinks in these texts. Early works on hypertext looked at the relationships between hyperlinks and the lexia they are linked to, with the assumption that good hyperlinks have clear sense relationships to lexia. This might be true for the everyday, non-fiction hyperlink found on most information websites, such as Wikipedia or the BBC News sites; however, the hyperlinks which connect lexia in hypertext fiction operate in a greater variety of ways. For Miles (2002, hypertext links have these functions: 'to facilitate navigation, allow cognitive and associative mapping of ideas, or the incorporation of otherwise disparate arguments, documents, or objects, within a larger contextualised docuverse'. Such variety of linking patterns could suggest that the connection between lexia holds a degree of the strength or weakness of association.

Given the complexity and possibilities for linking in hypertext, it is no surprise that many theorists have tackled this topic. Schneider (2005) suggests that the links between lexias tend to be looser than the links between paragraphs, and that readers are therefore not merely putting the pieces of a story together from the texts given to them. Readers often need to infer information, perhaps to a greater extent than they would when reading traditional printed literature.

These relationships between links and their effects on coherence and cohesion have led some theorists to suggest that hypertext is fiction, but not narrative; it is an alternative to narrative and can contain within it narration, which is true of other literary genres, such as poetry. We will see this illustrated in this chapter, in particular where we examine *Twelve Blue*. Similar comments are made by Miles (2002):

> In a poem you can place any word in any other location (as you can with shots in narrative cinema), and there is clearly no need for formal syntactic and semantic rules of organisation for a poem (or a film) to be meaningful – that there may be such rules for some genres of poetry does not change this fact.

This would certainly seem to be the case in hypertext and suggests that hypertext linking ought to be considered as more analogous to poetry than to prose.

Patchwork Girl

Landow describes Shelley Jackson's *Patchwork Girl* as a 'brilliant hypertext parable of writing and identity' which 'generates both its themes and techniques from the kinds of collage writing intrinsic in hypertext' (2006, p. 234). Approaching this hypertext from a social semiotic framework, we will be able to illustrate these characteristics of social meaning and their production. The field of the text is a story about a girl created from the body parts of others found in a graveyard. Such a premise immediately places the story into the genre of horror fiction, bringing to mind Mary Shelley's *Frankenstein*. The reader is also helped to make this intertextual reference by the title page, which plays with the similarities of the names Mary Shelley and Shelley Jackson by attributing authorship to 'Mary/Shelley & Herself'. While such references involve the sharing of background knowledge, which make up some of the interpersonal function, they can be seen as part of the ideational meaning as well; *Patchwork Girl* has been described as a 'rewriting' of *Frankenstein*. That is, the field conveys its meaning through its relationship to *Frankenstein* by taking the original Shelley plot and in some of the lexia actually rewriting passages of Shelley's text in the formal style of the nineteenth-century novel. In terms of cognitive approaches, we could say that mental representations are formed based on pre-existing knowledge and that these representations are modified by interacting with the new information provided in the text; the discourse world shared between author and reader, the knowledge of the *Frankenstein* story (which could come from film adaptations), is modified by the text world. But what makes this such a popular hypertext and enjoyable story to read is that the created human is female and is sewn together, literally in the text and metaphorically by the reader of the hypertext as each lexia is read. Moreover, the patchwork creation has twisted the original *Frankenstein* story, giving us a monster who is not feared by others and is mentally developed to the extent that she narrates portions of the story, often displaying a dry sense of humour.

Another aspect of the field of this text, which can be mapped to the discourse world in TWT, emerges from intertextual references to feminist theory and the children's book *The Patchwork Girl of Oz*, by L. Frank Baum. The lexia entitled 'scrap bag', for instance, includes passages quoted from feminist writer Barbara Stafford's book, *Body Criticism* and from Baum's other Oz books. As if to ensure the reader is aware of these references, Jackson includes sources within some of her lexia in a way more common to academic prose, giving a full reference list as a lexia hyperlinked to the title page. Such intertextuality helps to clarify the intended discourse world so that the story is read with a feminist perspective in mind and with a sense of a protagonist's journey as found in children's literature, which is consistent with Landow's comment about this being a 'parable'.

To describe the field more specifically, we can look to the text world with **world-building elements**, such as the settings of the graveyard and operating theatre as well as characters depicted in the various lexia. Even though a text world for a hypertext will vary from reader to reader, some general points can be made. Whatever sequence of lexia a given reader experiences, it is likely they set this story in the present day due to the occurrences of modern lexis. The main character is the eponymous patchwork girl or 'modern day monster', and many of the other characters are those whose body parts have been collected for the creation of the patchwork girl, such as the dancer whose trunk is used. The names of some of these women are found in an image lexia, called 'phrenology', shown in Figure 7.2.

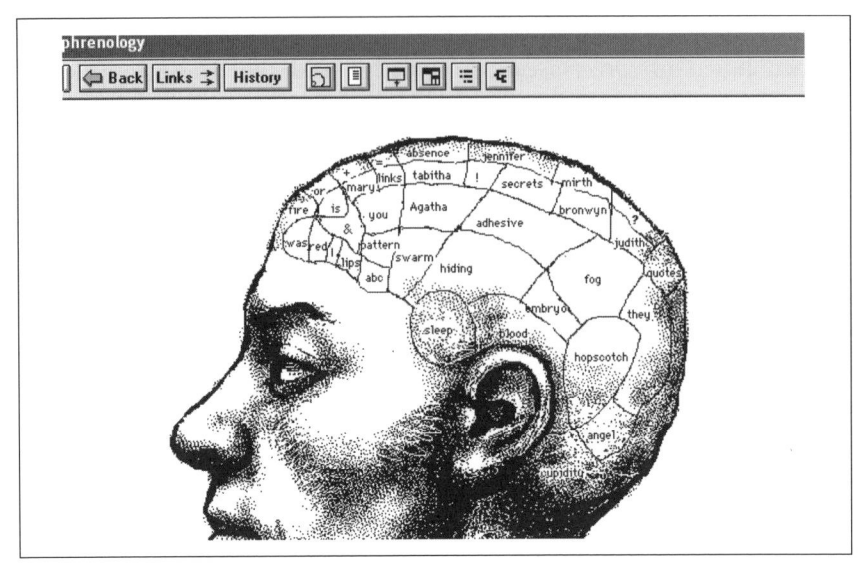

FIGURE 7.2 SCREEN IMAGE FROM *PATCHWORK GIRL*
Source: Jackson, S. (1995) *Patchwork Girl*. Watertown, MA: Eastgate Systems

Here, a profile of a head is divided into sections labelled with either women's names or single words or symbols which help to advance the narrative. By clicking on each woman's name, a lexia appears with her story, saying which body part she has contributed to the patchwork girl; through other lexia the reader also discovers body parts from men and an intestine taken from Bossy, a cow. Another main character in the story is Mary, assumed to be Mary Shelley, who is described by the patchwork girl as her 'lover, friend, collaborator'. These characters constitute world-building elements which could be described as also being **function-advancing propositions**. Ensslin (2007) notes elements and propositions coming together when she describes this hypertext as 'a story which features a female monster on her quest for a new, a-gendered space for creative self-expression' (p. 79).

The interpersonal function of the text as discourse communicated between author and reader can be observed in several ways. The shared knowledge of Mary Shelley's *Frankenstein* makes the configuration of this patchwork creature somewhat comical, as does some of the storytelling itself. Moreover, the tenor of the text is composed of different lexia being written in different registers of formality and communicating in either first or third person perspectives; in one lexia, called 'interrupting D', the reader is presented with a transcript of someone interviewing the patchwork girl. We also have here an interesting use of the second person, where *you* refers to the reader as navigator through the story: 'I am buried here. You can resurrect me, but only in piecemeal. If you want to see me whole you will have to sew me together yourself'. This instruction uses the metaphor of sewing, with the reader being asked to click and read their way through the story, where reading is like sewing as it brings the pieces of the body and the story together.

As described in Chapter 6, world-switching occurs within the text world and can appear to readers as flashbacks or flashforwards, depending on the order in which various lexia are read. The reader sees from the title page that the story is divided into five main sections: 'a graveyard', 'a journal', 'a quilt', 'a story', '& broken accents', followed by a section entitled '(sources)'. These sections suggest an order of reading for the simple reasons that '&' appears before the last main section listed and 'sources' at the very end; however, the navigational map of this story, in Figure 7.3, shows which lexia are linked to each other, but seems to suggest a free ordering of time for recreating the patchwork girl. In other words, each reader experiences the creation of various text worlds differently within it.

Modal worlds might be identified in this story by the desires and beliefs of characters and hypothetical worlds set out by the narrators.

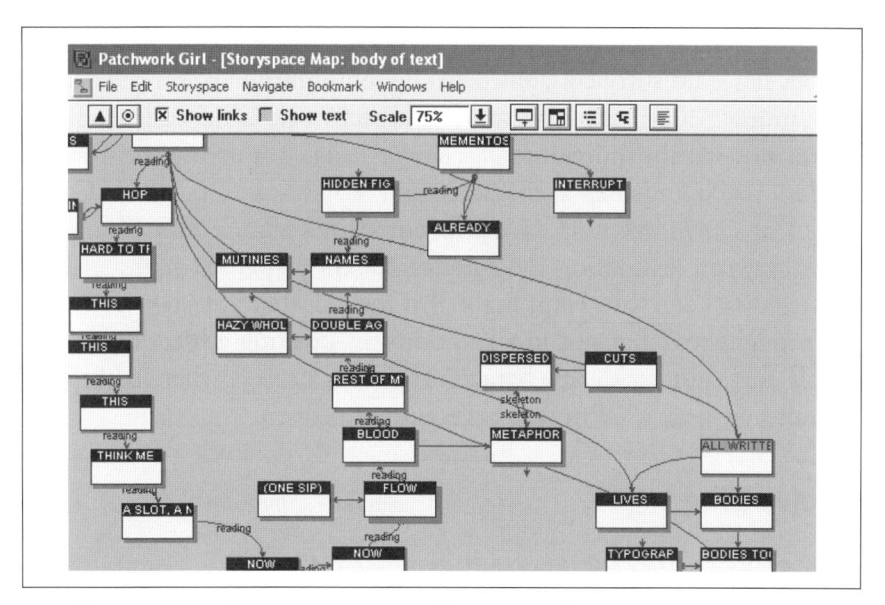

FIGURE 7.3 SCREEN IMAGE FROM *PATCHWORK GIRL* SHOWING STORY MAP
Source: Jackson, S. (1995) *Patchwork Girl*. Watertown, MA: Eastgate Systems

An example of this appears in the lexia entitled 'this writing', where the text reveals the monster's state-of-mind due to her own sense of incompleteness:

> Assembling these patched words in an electronic space, I feel half-blind, as if the entire text is within reach, but because of some myopic condition I am only familiar with from dreams, I can only see the part immediately before me, and have no sense of how that part relates to the rest.

Within the textual function of this particular hypertext, the mode includes identifiable links as dictated by the sections of the title page and the navigational map, both referred to above. Moreover, the software presentation of *Patchwork Girl* includes buttons listing which lexia the reader has already experienced, as well as the other lexia the current screen links to. The reader is also able to achieve coherence of the texts through the various themes which relate to the environment of this story; in several readings of *Patchwork Girl*, the narrator-as-subject has yielded the themes of identity, gender and homosexuality (Hayles, 2000; Landow, 2006). In addition, the repetition of themes and phrases, as well as supporting images of body parts, helps readers to create a unified whole even if the sequence of reading is individual. Yet at the same time, the sense of cohesion and coherence for this work is not strong or clear for the reader. Sometimes the linking of lexia provides a likely continuation of a narrative chain, but at other times it does not, and story coherence can be temporarily lost on the reader. As Landow (2006) explains, 'most of Patchwork Girls' collage effects occur, not within individual patches or lexia, but across them as we readers patch together a character and a narrative' (p. 236). Other critics of *Patchwork Girl* have also noted this feature, describing the links between lexia using the language of the hypertext itself, such as *sutures*, *seams* and *scars*. This highlights the fact that links between lexia are brought together not in a smooth way, creating a blending into a whole text, but in a way characteristic of hypertext wherein the text will always show itself to be a collection of parts.

Twelve Blue

Unlike *Patchwork Girl*, *Twelve Blue*, as its title suggests, employs colours as part of the reading experience in the form of both words and images. The opening screen consists of 12 lines, appearing as if on a line graph, where some lines intersect each other; each line is a different colour, mostly blue, one purple, one pink and one yellow. Most importantly, each of these lines contains a link to a lexia of the story. Depending on one's reading, a lexia occurs later in the story which reflects this image in words:

> She looked out on the creek and measured out the threads like the fates, silk travel in twelve shades of blue. (Is pink blue? Is yellow or purple? She supposed so, she believed in her stories.)

If the reader chooses to click on the link which provides instructions for reading this hypertext, they are greeted with only a limited idea of the linking structure, thus revealing a restricted sense of reader empowerment:

> The story threads quite obviously along its edges, like frayed cloth, in the left window. You'll find links there. There are passing links within the text on the right as well, but these, once followed, go away. You'll want, I think, to open the space so all twelve threads show, diurnally (a not terribly obscure word for the weaving and unraveling of time) […] Twelve blue isn't anything. Think of lilacs when they're gone.

The ways in which the storylines weave together and later unravel, sometimes coming together later in new ways, can be described by two other terms which come from TWT: world repair and world replacement. First introduced into TWT by Gavins (2000), world repair and world replacement can apply to any type of discourse and are particularly useful here. World repair occurs when world-building elements or function-advancing propositions have been miscommunicated or misunderstood and the reader realises this and corrects it by altering their conceptualisation of those elements of texts. In some cases world repair is not enough for the reader to make sense of the world they are trying to construct, in which case a world replacement occurs. For many readers of *Twelve Blue,* world repair is necessary when one character is mistaken for another because of the use of pronouns instead of names. Moreover, sometimes the same character is referred to by a different name; in these cases, the reader's discovery of the character having two names results in the need to replace two different worlds inhabited by two characters with a single world containing one character with two names.

When the reader starts *Twelve Blue*, some aspects of the social and cultural context might be shared with this contemporary author, but the opening screen provides little else in the way of social or cultural cues. But a few lexia into the story and the reader has already surmised that this fiction takes place in the last part of the twentieth century and mostly in North America. The discourse world shared between writer and reader is not as intertextual as we saw with *Patchwork Girl* and is somewhat limited for the reader at the start of the reading experience.

The field, as with any hypertext, will vary in its particulars from reader to reader, but some points can be made in terms of characters and places depicted across the lexia, which can be mapped in TWT to world-building elements. There are several characters referred to by name and others by description, such as the drowned boy and the drowned woman. The settings of the worlds within the text world include several places across North America, including Canada, upstate New York and the Blue Mountains of Australia. The field of the story broadly covers the lives and relationships between these characters and their memories of two deaths by drowning and a murder. But articulating the field of the story in this way might be misleading; as noted in Ryan (2001): 'The text is not a whodunit, and the motivation of its main events is better found in symbolism and textual architecture than in the particular interests of the characters' (p. 236).

Given this use of symbolism, it could also be said that ideational and textual functions work together in creating meaning for this hypertext. For readers of *Twelve Blue*, the opening screen has a blue background, like all of the screens in this hypertext, and numbered hyperlinks suggesting a narrative order or at least an order in which to experience the text. As noted earlier, the story is presented on the first navigation page as a 'story in eight bars', and each 'bar' seems to lead to a section of the story. By moving the cursor randomly across the first screen, the reader can also find hidden hyperlinks along one of the margins of the screen, hidden in the coloured waves. For the written text within a hypertext fiction, this covers the characters and main story. This, however, is by no means straightforward; consider this lexia:

> Samantha walked down to the edge of the creek where the spongy earth ceased in a scum fringe like the edge of a dark carpet. The shore smelled like potting soil or something more familiar, the smell of blood sometimes at your period.

It was ripe water her mother said once. Already the water chestnuts began to grow beneath the black surface of the water. They would grow into another carpet, an emerald one extending from the scum fringe to the opposite shore of the estuary.

Ripe and riparian.

There was an image of the sky inside the ebony water, a scoop of blue and tufts of feathery white, the reflection floating there like a damp photograph.

She was startled by a swimmer surfacing exactly in the patch of blue where the photograph floated. He was a skinny boy, naked and white as soap, the hollows of his buttocks as blue as photographs. The boy smoothed his black hair straight back against his skull. It was black as tar and shined like the water. He smiled and showed uneven teeth. His eyes were wary.

His name was Henry Stone and he had come back to her.

It is a good story, her mother said, I like how the earth smells like blood.

The final sentence of this lexia triggers a world-switch to another story, referring to an earlier portion of the lexia as 'a good story' and commenting on the story by repeating the phrase 'smells like blood'. This story within the story creates two text worlds, rich in themes which hold together the otherwise non-linear and multilinear hypertext. For some readers this world switch to a character narrating the story might be an instance of world repair, as a misunderstanding could initially occur when reading the final line with its lack of quotation marks to indicate another speaker.

As noted when describing the field of the text, the many characters and their relationships contribute to the reader's rendering of a text world. World-switching occurs as readers interact with lexia which appear to be memories, flashbacks, flashforwards, or stories within the story, as in the example above. Miles (2006) notes that '[…] it is common for a [hypertext] narrative event or element to shift from an apparently minor to a major role (or the reverse) subject to our interpretation of later events and how we then apply these to our original schema'. As with *Patchwork Girl*, readers' experiences can be described in terms of world-building or world-switching, depending on the order of reading various lexia. The narration of the story is written in a way so as to suggest a verbal retelling from an unclear memory, perhaps being reconstructed as the story is told. In this hypertext, these separate worlds are sometimes distinguished in lexia where characters have changed their names or where they used a nickname in childhood; these different names indicate a point in the distant past.

The ways in which text worlds are developed in this hypertext, with stories retold and recalled through internal dialogue, lend themselves to a description of the textual meaning, in which the presentation of story fragments bears upon the meanings we give to the text. Further to this, we can consider how the reader might interact with the text, moving between the lexia, and how coherence and cohesion might be achieved. Within *Twelve Blue* many lexia have multiple links for the reader to choose from, and as mentioned earlier these are more explicit links, which help to make the text coherent. This suggests that to some extent the readers actually create some of the textual function themselves, as how they read the story depends on the choices they make. Moreover, the lexia also tend to have strong lexically cohesive elements, such as direct repetition, synonyms and hyponyms, making it obvious that the narrative continues through different lexia, though not usually chronologically. Table 7.1 illustrates this, with the three lexia entitled *fates*, *riven wishes* and *white moths*.

Similarly, textual arrangement creating the structure of this particular hypertext, no matter what order the lexia are read in, simulates the associative workings typical of human memory. This feature has also been noted in Michael Joyce's canonical hypertext *afternoon*. Ensslin comments on the way writers have used the affordances of hypertext 'for the representation of conscious and subconscious cognitive processes such as memory, learning, imagination, dream, fantasy and nightmare' (Ensslin, 2012, p. 140).

As semiotic and cognitive approaches have shown, *Twelve Blue*, can be a challenging hypertext to read, or 'experience' as some readers

TABLE 7.1 LEXICAL COHESION ACROSS THREE LEXIA IN *TWELVE BLUE*

Type of lexical cohesion	Fates	Riven wishes	White moths
Direct repetition	Colour threads death	Colour threads death	Death
Synonyms	Shades of blue	Bluish water	Tears
Hyponyms	Colour drowned boy	Bluish water	White

might say. But it does serve to demonstrate the salience of the features of reader empowerment, linearity and cohesion and coherence when examining such digital texts.

> **Activity**
>
> Ensslin notes that '[…] the overall "confusion" in the reader caused by hypertextuality, nonlinearity and non-closure contributes to the narrator's unreliability' (Ensslin, 2012, p. 140) and a tendency for hypertext narratives to be presented through the vehicles of dreams, memories and the inner thoughts of a possibly unreliable narrator. Consider the extent to which this might be true of *Patchwork Girl* and *Twelve Blue*, based on your own reading experience of these texts.

'Samantha in Winter'

'Samantha in Winter' is a third person narrative recounting episodes in the life of Samantha, an anxious teenage girl with decisions to make about her boyfriend, Mark, and her future studies and career. What makes it a short story is the fact that it contains far fewer lexia (only 14) than typical hypertext novels, which contain hundreds of lexia. Unlike the other hypertext fictions discussed in this chapter, 'Samantha in Winter' does not include images or the use of colour. Typical lexia in this story are made of three paragraphs of text with one to five hyperlinks to other lexia.

The field and elements of the text world include the episodes and descriptions of people in Samantha's life, with friends and family as key characters. In this example lexia, Samantha describes her mother and the worrying that goes on in her family over her future:

> Sam's mum called her Samantha when she wanted to show disapproval, or that she was being really serious. She'd been calling her that a lot recently. Sam's way of getting back was to call her 'Mother' but she wasn't sure it worked; her mum seemed to quite like it.
>
> Sam's mum was worried about her all the time – worried that she wouldn't go to university, worried that she would, worried that <u>biology</u> was too difficult a subject, worried that she took it too seriously. Mark worried her too – were he and Sam not serious enough, or was it so serious that she'd put off university to stay with him? Everything was serious, everything worried her.

> And always the same reason for her worry – 'Samantha, make something of your life, don't waste it, don't end up like….' Like her, of course, but why was that so bad? At night, when she was studying in her room, Sam could hear her mum worrying about her to her <u>dad</u>, complaining because he wasn't worried too. Sometimes Sam's mum worried her.

Drawing a further analysis from TWT, we could say that the above lexia helps to create a text world about Sam which in part comes from a discourse world which might include pre-existing knowledge of typical teenage anxiety.

As we can also see from the example lexia, modal worlds are particularly salient in this short work. Most of the lexia contain deontic modality in the form of wishes and fears about an imagined future, expressed above in 'Sam's mum worried her'. But here, using the affordances of hypertexts, other modal worlds emerge – for instance, if the reader clicks on 'biology', they are sent to another lexia entitled 'biology'; in this lexia, Samantha's true feelings towards studying biology are revealed. Using different lexia in this way, two Samanthas appear: a storytelling Samantha, who is an unreliable narrator, and an inner Samantha, who expresses more genuine feelings.

As we can see from the example text and discussion so far, the relationship between hyperlinked words and the lexia they lead to have strong semantic associations. Clicking on 'biology' or 'dad' gives the reader a lexia about each of these things. It could be said that here reader empowerment is rather strong as the reader can make informed choices about what they wish to read next.

From this example, the interpersonal function of the language emerges from within the text world and between writer and reader. The direct and indirect speech between mother and daughter show their status to each other in ways typical in the actual world; for example, Samantha's awareness of the relationship when referring to her mother as 'Mother'. Looking at this passage in terms of its tenor as a text being communicated to a reader, the informal register and vernacular word choice make the text appear as if written by Samantha, or certainly within her understanding of the world.

In terms of textual function, without images, the only mode is the written word. Unlike *Patchwork Girl* and *Twelve Blue*, there is no sort of navigation page to suggest an arrangement or ordering of lexia. The textual function can be observed through the reader's experience of links to lexia and lexical cohesion found in the content of the lexia. The reader's experience of clicking on links is guided by key words at the top of the screen and set out in such a way that readers can retrace their steps and reread lexia. In addition, cohesion for this story is found across lexia by use of repetition of names of characters, as opposed to the use of ambiguous pronouns sometimes found in other hypertext fictions. Hyponyms, relating, for instance, university and biology, or mother with father, across lexia also give the text as a whole cohesion. Another cohesive device used by authors is often referred to as an ordered series, such as *first, second, third*, or seasons, *spring* and *summer*. In this hypertext the ordered series of seasons and time also play a key role in making this hypertext cohesive and coherent. Moreover, a lexia entitled 'next year' is experienced late in the reading experience, due to the lexia which it is linked with. This combination of lexical cohesion in expecting a time after the spring and summer lexia, along with the technical positioning of this 'next year' lexia, has been perceived by some readers as yielding a sense of closure.

Such textual features make this story more coherent and cohesive than the longer hypertext fictions such as *Patchwork Girl* and *Twelve Blue*. With the short number of lexia and ways of retracing steps, unlike the novel-length hypertext discussed earlier, the non-linearity of the narrative is less problematic or frustrating for the reader. Moreover, with so few lexia the different narratives presented, which in this case seems to be one central one, appear less convoluted. Such features may very well distinguish short stories from novel-length hypertext.

Activity

Read another hypertext short story, such as 'Lies' by Rick Pryll (http://users.rcn.com/rick.interport/lies/lies.html). Using an SFL framework, discuss the similarities and differences between your chosen short story and 'Samantha in Winter'.

Conclusions

In addition to introducing the ways in which hypertexts operate, this chapter has outlined analyses of three hypertext fictions. By employing social semiotic approaches, the ways in which these texts are communicated between writer and reader have been discussed within a workable paradigm. We have, for example, considered the tenor of these texts in terms of author to reader interaction and the use of different registers. The mode in which these texts communicate challenges ideas of document design and the arrangements of sections of texts, as we are more accustomed to reading the printed page and fiction presented in the form of books. As these texts have all been narratives, the ideational function of language and its related field component of texts have been approached more specifically using TWT. As we found with networked novels in the previous chapter, the categories of TWT, such as discourse worlds and modal worlds, are useful for describing stories which do not follow completely linear planes and stories which might be multilinear, yet are connected by shared worlds. Moreover, here world-switching, world repair and world replacement help to explain the complexity of such texts.

There is much debate about the future of hypertext fiction. For some, hypertext allows for literary and artistic expression of our technically changing times. Others still see hypertext fiction as part of a larger system of communication and learning which has pedagogical implications, making it ripe for the literary canon as well as a way of developing critical thinking, as found in Ensslin (2007). Moreover, hypertext fiction has its detractors, who claim that this form of literature is no more than a novelty, enjoyed more by academics than 'ordinary' readers. Other criticisms of the hypertext reading experience, which perhaps you have experienced yourself if you have read any of the hypertext fictions mentioned in this chapter, have to do with the hypertext medium as a reading experience. On the one hand, the difference between reading a printed book compared with reading on a screen and having to find and click hyperlinks to advance the story for what can be a considerable amount of time, and on the other hand, the challenge of reading a text, which unlike a book, is not in a predictable design format.

Sample projects

1. In this chapter, the analyses outlined have been based on the reading experiences of my students and me. After reading, and

probably rereading, one of these texts, apply your own TWT analysis. Consider how similar or different your experience and resulting analysis are to those presented here.

2. Now that you have read some hypertext fictions, write about your personal experiences and opinions on these points:

   a. How did you feel about reading lengthy works on a computer screen?

   b. Did you feel more empowered as a reader of hypertext than you have felt reading printed novels?

   c. How did you feel about reading texts which perhaps did not have an ending or sense of closure?

Further reading

In addition to the books listed below, academic articles on hypertext fiction can be found in journals in media studies, such as *Convergence*, and in linguistics and literature journals, such as *Narrative* and *The Journal of English Studies*.

Aarseth, E. J. (1997) *Cybertext: Perspectives on Ergodic Literature.* Baltimore: The Johns Hopkins University Press.

This is one of the earlier books on hypertext, but worth reading for its criticism of structuralist and post-structuralist approaches to hypertext. Aarseth's study of hypertext is rooted in gaming theory and provides analysis on the role of the reader as hypertext participant.

Bell, A. (2010) *The Possible Worlds of Hypertext Fiction.* Basingstoke: Palgrave Macmillan.

This book offers analyses of the major Storyspace hypertext fictions, including *Patchwork Girl*, employing possible worlds theory which rests within cognitive approaches.

Ensslin, A. (2007) *Canonizing Hypertext: Explorations and Constructions.* London: Continuum.

This book looks at the pedagogical possibilities for using hypertext fiction in the same way we study print literatures. It debates the aesthetic and literary qualities of these texts, drawing from linguistics and literary criticism.

Landow, G. (2006) *Hypertext 3.0: Critical Theory and New Media in an Era of Globalization.* Baltimore: Johns Hopkins University Press.

Mentioned in previous chapters and considered by many to be the Bible of hypertext theory, this third edition of Landow's original work provides an overview of media and literary theories about hypertext. Its chapter on hypertext narrative includes sections devoted to Storyspace fiction, such as *Patchwork Girl*.

Websites used in this chapter

Joyce, M. (1996) *Twelve Blue,* http://www.eastgate.com/TwelveBlue/

Stephens, P. (2004) Samantha in Winter, http://www.paulspages.co.uk/htext/saminwinter.htm

8 Genre Hybrids and Superdiversity

Introduction

Throughout this book we have seen new text types and discourse structures which have arisen using the affordances of digital communication, such as those found in chat rooms, collaborative fiction and j-blogs. Here we re-examine these new text types, along with introducing a few others, in terms of genre and considering the extent to which they can be seen as hybrids of existing genres. Just as digital communication has created new genres, new styles of discourse have emerged in online environments. We mentioned in Chapter 1 that digital talk can involve using acronyms and punctuation to create emoticons, as well as using pre-created emoji images. Here, we extend our understanding of digital talk by looking at the concept of **superdiversity** and how it is being applied to the development of language use online. To better understand genre hybridity and superdiversity, we will examine a blog which serves as an example of both concepts. These investigations into developments and changes to text structures and language styles naturally bring us to reconsider different theoretical approaches to digital textuality.

Upon completion of this chapter you will be able to describe digital texts in terms of genre hybrids; this will involve an understanding of related terms, such as interdiscursivity. You will also be able to describe chosen texts with respect to superdiversity and how this concept relates to code-mixing and style-shifting. As this is a concluding chapter with a review of key theoretical points, you should also have a more complete understanding of the theoretical issues and directions for further research in the study of digital textuality, which may include your own.

Genres

Throughout this book we have used the term **genre**, assuming a basic linguistic understanding of what is meant by it. Here we will look more closely at the concept of genre and the nature of new genres brought about through digital communication. Generally, when we use the term genre we are talking about structured and conventionalised forms of texts. For instance, genre is used to distinguish poetry from fictional prose, as these two text types are structured differently and follow different lexico-grammatical conventions. In linguistics we extend this basic idea. Going beyond the rhetorical structure and conventions for the production of texts by placing the idea of genre into its social context. Such a perspective was briefly mentioned in Chapter 3, where we noted John Swales' (1990) use of genre to refer to a communicative event, characterised by a set of communicative purposes. In a similar vein, Martin (1984) describes genre in an SFL framework, placing it into a sociocultural context, as 'a staged, goal-orientated, and purposeful social activity that people engage in as members of their culture' (p. 25). Encapsulating these different approaches to the study of genre as involving both linguistic form and sociocultural purpose, Bhatia (2004) offers the following definition:

> Genre essentially refers to language use in a conventionalised communicative setting in order to give expression to a specific set of communicative goals of a disciplinary or social institution, which give rise to stable structural forms by imposing constraints on the use of lexico-grammatical as well as discoursal resources. (p. 23)

This definition brings together the idea of genre as a textual structure with that of genre as a way of fulfilling communicative purposes. Using this definition, we can categorise and delineate texts in ways which clarify and enrich our understanding of digital texts. For instance, we could describe the textuality of fiction printed in books in relation to the hypertext fiction we examined in the last chapter. Both are genres of fiction and share some of the stabilised structural forms such as descriptive narration and the quoted speech of characters; however, their different communicative goals and social contexts give rise to distinguishing textual features The communicative goal for hypertext fiction to be more reader interactive and unique to different readers' experiences of discovering lexia is related to its structural conventions; for example, the ways in which hypertext fictions break down texts in lexia giving it a different structural convention to printed fiction.

We can also explore genre to highlight the differences between digital talk and face-to-face talk. Chat room discourse is its own unique speech genre as it uses abbreviations, emoticons and emoji, generic conventions which could not occur in face-to-face talk. These differences have arisen out of the discoursal resources at hand, as well as from the different communicative purposes, such as the need to produce written responses quickly (which would not apply to oral talk by definition). While both genres might have similar social purposes, writing talk in a chat room also carries with it the purpose of identity performance amongst strangers, for which abbreviations and emoticons can express personal style and creativity. As we can see, Bhatia's two-layered definition of genre accounts for the relationships between linguistic and textual structures and the purposes of communication.

Current linguistic scholarship of online genres has treated different platforms as creators of different genres. For example, we have treated SNSs as a type of genre, as the features of such platforms, such as profile pages, likes and comments, manifest shared linguistic conventions. These features are related to general purposes in communication shared among SNSs, namely to socialise and maintain relationships. We can also see different platforms and their technological affordances giving rise to genres in the cases of collaborative fiction as discussed in Chapter 6 and the hypertext fiction from Chapter 7. Both of these digital text types share the general characteristics found in fictional prose, yet their technological platforms yield different communicative events. With its use of comments, the Ficly.com collaborative fiction site could be seen as having social and critical purposes expressed in registers different from those found in their fictional prose and different from what we usually find in hypertext fiction. Another point for consideration are the communicative functions in the use of storytelling, which go across various genre-defined platforms. This case is made by Page (2012), who investigates storytelling in social media, noting that fictional storytelling is not only found in sites such as those described in Chapters 6 and 7, but also in blogs, life writing and a range of SNSs.

It also needs to be said that distinct genres can emerge from within a platform in ways not dictated by the technologies, but instead through cultural understandings. For example, SNSs can differ in their specific purposes which impact upon the linguistic conventions and structures of the texts involved. We gave the example in Chapter 3 of how profiles in LinkedIn differ from those found in Facebook in terms of register and lexico-grammatical features; looking at this through the lens of genres, we can say that these sites have different purposes, which are culturally understood. Users of LinkedIn associate the site with professions and careers, whereas Facebook is understood to be used for more personalised socialising. While we broadly refer to LinkedIn and Facebook as examples of SNSs, generically they belong to different subgenres.

An understanding of genre can also be used to refine our classification of other types of digital texts discussed in earlier chapters. Where some of the texts we examined required interactivity, they could be understood as having a different purpose than those texts not intended to be interactive; this is, of course, bearing in mind that any reading of a text is in some sense interactive on the part of readers as they engage with texts. For instance, in Chapter 2 we looked at informal learning brought about through the use of Wikipedia; most of us who refer to and read Wikipedia as a potential source of information are not interacting with the text beyond skimming or reading it, unlike the writers who are contributing to it. This differs from informal learning, as found in the school revision sites, where interaction is required, such as providing answers to questions and filling in grids and diagrams. Noting these different communicative purposes, and indeed in these cases, very different communicative events, helps us to articulate generic differences. While Wikipedia and the school revision sites might share linguistic registers and structures, such as semi-formal language and passive sentences, the interactivity can give rise to questions and note-form answers, as well as shorter, self-contained texts. Another example where interactivity helps to define genres could be seen in the digital poetry discussed in Chapter 5, where poems which required readers to click on texts and images in order to reveal other texts and images had a different communicative purpose than the animated digital poetry found on YouTube. Different textual structures occur in these cases as a result of meaning being created to some extent by the reader's choices instead of animation brought on by the production of the text. In this case, the generic differences may seem somewhat subtle, as other linguistic features unite these poems as poetic writing, in contrast to prose writing. Moreover, these poems share communicative purposes, which as we pointed out earlier could be described in terms of **Jakobson's functions of language**, as having poetic and emotive functions.

Genre hybrids

One of the most discussed characteristics of digital texts has been the emergence of genre hybrids, the routine mixing of genres to produce new genres. SNSs, for example, are not all strictly 'social' as their name suggests; we find other genres embedded within SNSs having communicative purposes other than socialising. When advertisers use social media, the generic conventions follow those of advertising. Quite often the language and text structures bear resemblance to their non-digital counterparts. For example, advertisements for electronic goods which appear on manufacturers' Facebook pages are likely to resemble pages of a catalogue, not just in their arrangement of texts and images, but also in their lexico-grammatical features and register; we would likely find bullet-point descriptions and the use of a technical register understood by the purchasing public. Some advertisers use sites such as Facebook and Twitter to upload video clips about their products and services. These clips are often extended television commercials, following the same generic conventions of television advertising. In such cases the notable differences to traditional paper-based or television advertising are not so much language or textual structure as they are the use of internet affordances, such as the ability to scroll down a page of product advertisements, mixing still images with video clips, along with hyperlinks to the checkout basket.

These examples of essentially social media advertising can also be described by what Norman Fairclough refers to as 'interdiscursivity'.

This is defined as 'the mixing configuration of discourse conventions such as genres, activity types, and styles associated with different types of discourse' (Fairclough, 1992, p. 84). That is, they are mixing a social media genre with styles of language associated with other genres to do with advertising. Interdiscursivity is often defined in relation to **intertextuality**, as Fairclough himself first introduced the new term interdiscursivity to replace the term 'constitutive intertextuality', a borrowing of discourse conventions and styles. This is distinguished from 'manifest intertextuality', which refers to the explicit borrowing of texts and placing them in another text. A text such as *Patchwork Girl*, which we examined in Chapter 7, is rich in examples of intertextuality (i.e., manifest intertextuality) and interdiscursivity (or constitutive intertextuality). As we noted in *Patchwork Girl*, intertextual references included those to Mary Shelley's *Frankenstein* and Frank Baum's *The Patchwork Girl of Oz*; examples of interdiscursivity include the lexia which read like academic criticism and those lexia which copy the style and some of the wording of Shelley's nineteenth-century text.

Similarly, we saw in Chapter 4 examples of genre hybridity and interdiscursivity where Twitter has been used by professional journalists and laypeople to communicate news stories. In the tweets by professional journalists, the styles of writing found in journalism tend to be followed, with a tendency towards headline writing in order to accommodate the constraints of 140 characters. Some sports journalists have used Twitter to provide ongoing commentaries of live sporting events, producing language which follows some of the conventions of radio reporting; the fact that this is accomplished in writing suggests a form of digital talk and some sort of hybrid genre, bringing together radio sports commentaries with journalistic headline writing. News stories tweeted by laypeople (non-journalists) could also be said to form another hybrid genre, where these are used to express the views of the writer. Consider the two example tweets below.

1. 'Medical students from low performing schools do better, study finds' (link to study included).
2. 'LMHR gig goes ahead despite previous gig being shut down by EDL and police. Well done to organisers' (links and photograph included).

The first example is from the tweet of Paul Jump, a journalist for *Times Higher Education*, writing in his own Twitter account, but writing in a style similar to news headlines; this is marked by placing the prominent information first and by using the phrase 'study finds', which commonly occurs in journalistic writing. The second example also has the purpose of providing news and uses a headline writing style, but is written by a non-journalist and includes a brief commentary in the second sentence.

While online news is rich in genre hybridity, it can also be treated as one genre, where the dissemination of news and commentary is the main purpose of these sites. Users are free to participate as readers only of the news presented. Within this genre of news, there are naturally subgenres with distinct registers and textual structures; for example, the business and sports sections vary in terms specific to those fields and in the presentation of texts with stock listings and scoreboards. As we saw in Chapter 4, these sites also have other more social purposes. For instance, the use of comments with each article published online allows readers to interact with each other as well as with the authors of articles; these comments can follow the conventions of digital talk or opinion writing found in digital texts. In addition to this, users engage in social activities brought on by the inclusion of social media links and icons. For example, any story read at the BBC website can be shared with others via Facebook, Twitter and LinkedIn, along with direct links to social bookmarking sites Delicious, Reddit and StumbleUpon. These sites have direct interfaces so that users do not need to sign into their own accounts. Given this ease of linking news to social networking, such sites can be seen as belonging to a hybrid genre, as language conventions are altered with purpose. For example, commentaries on news articles saved and shared in Delicious add to the linked article opinions, sometimes with persuasive language and attitudinal stances.

As many of the examples in this section come from SNSs, it is worth noting that current research in SNSs acknowledges the importance of genre hybridity in analysing SNSs. According to Page (2012), 'Social media is characterized by complex forms of hybridity and intertextuality, where the boundaries of generic and textual contexts become porous, and bleed into other sites through parody, hyperlinks, and quotation'. Further examples of this can be found in the many 'fake' blog pages of fictional characters and Twitter accounts, such as the one referred to in Chapter 3, supposedly producing tweets from God.

> **Activity**
>
> Visit the following website with the poem 'Riddles' by Nick Montfort: http://www.studiocleo.com/cauldron/volume4/confluence/montfort/riddles.html. Try to answer the riddles yourself in this interactive poem. Consider the extent to which this poem belongs to the genres of poetry and riddles; in doing this, include linguistic features and the purposes of this text as a communicative event.

Urban Dictionary

Here we are taking a brief look at Urban Dictionary, which provides examples of genre hybridity and interdiscursivity. This online dictionary is a web-based reference source which, like Wikipedia, relies on text contributions from the public. It describes itself as 'a veritable cornucopia of streetwise lingo, posted and defined by its readers'. As of 2013, it claimed to contain definitions for over seven million words in English. The dictionary as a whole can be treated as a genre hybrid, bringing together a dictionary with wiki-style collaboration and interactive social media features, such as 'like' icons and comments. Many of the definitions follow the linguistic and structural conventions associated with dictionaries. For example, the definition for *tool* is as follows: 'One who lacks the mental capacity to know he is being used. A fool. A cretin. Characterized by low intelligence and/or self-esteem'. This definition follows the linguistic style of traditional dictionaries by using fragmented sentences and having a general classification, followed by a specific distinguishing feature; that is, 'one' tells us that it applies to people (as opposed to things) and 'who lacks the mental capacity [...]' tells us how the term refers to a specific type of person. After this definition an example is provided, which also follows the structure of many traditional dictionaries. But after this, the entry diverts from the dictionary genre with SNS sharing icons, a YouTube clip making fun of tools and a link to where readers can buy 'tool' t-shirts. This blending of social media and the contributions of readers, often employing different registers, makes this a hybrid genre which is highly **heteroglossic**.

In another example for Urban Dictionary, the book *The Perks of Being a Wallflower* by Stephen Chbosky is an actual dictionary entry; this in itself does not follow the genre conventions of traditional dictionaries, which usually do not define contemporary fiction. For this entry, site visitors have used the 'comments' option in a way similar to microblogging, with recommendations and evaluations of these books as a whole, as can be seen in the comments below:

1. An amazing book about a boy who is a wallflower in high school. It is written in letters when he befriends a gay guy and his sister, who he falls in love with […]
2. A book for anyone who feels disconnected, unable to connect, alone/lonely, unappreciated and sad. The story of a boy named Charlie and his most intimate thoughts shared with an anonymous friend by letter […] a must read for anyone sensitive […]

These two so-called 'definitions' follow the format of SNSs in allowing readers to rank the definitions, with number 1 being the most liked, as well as giving comments, which are themselves treated as if part of the definition. As this format duplicates the style of other social media sites, it suggests another type of platform for discussing books online. In this environment, unlike some of the social media sites, the synopses in these comments are apparent ways of trying to make the commentaries about the book appear more informative within this dictionary genre and at the same time evaluative, which would not be expected of dictionaries. It could also be described as interdiscursive, as these brief synopses follow some of the styles and discourse conventions of 'blurbs' found on the jackets of books. In addition, the entry also includes the quote below from the book:

> I don't know if you ever felt like that. That you wanted to sleep for a thousand years. Or just not exist. Or just not be aware that you do exist. Or something like that.

This use of a quote is also a convention of book reviews, which gives the review reader a flavour of the prose style and the attitude of the narrator.

> **Activity**
>
> Go to the Urban Dictionary (http://www.urbandictionary.com) and look up the word *wicked*. Analyse the definitions provided in terms of genre hybridity. Identify occurrences of interdiscursivity and the extent to which the entire definition is heteroglossic.

Digital essays

Here we will examine another type of genre hybrid, which can also be considered in terms of intertextuality and interdiscursivity. Student essay writing has taken on new forms since the inception of the internet, with a variety of ways of using the affordances of digital technologies. At one end of the digital spectrum are essays close to the traditionally printed ones, where students produce essays through word-processing software and upload them online for their teachers to mark. These texts use some of the affordances of digital platforms by, for example, providing hyperlinks in their reference pages, allowing teachers to access a source work directly through the internet. In software such as Word, the teacher can also leave typewritten comments directly on the text. While these differences to printed versions of essays add a few textual features, the textual structures and the communicative purposes remains more or less the same; that is, these digital texts could be said to belong to the same genre as traditionally printed texts. At the other end of the digital spectrum are student essays which incorporate animation and interactive features, along with additional modes of sound and spoken language. With essays such as these, different textual structures emerge, which make them examples of hybrid genres. Moreover, while the communicative purposes might share some points with traditional essays, they might also have other purposes, including to entertain and to demonstrate digital skills (the latter of which could be a criterion in their assessment by the teacher). In this section we will examine one such hybrid essay; two others can be found in Sample Projects at the end of this chapter.

Postgraduate student Andy Murray produced a digital essay in a video platform about digital essays and digital learning environments for his MA in E-Learning and Digital Culture. The video runs for nearly 20 minutes and incorporates the modes of spoken and written language along with visual images and music. This essay belongs to the genre of student essays in as much as it has the communicative purposes of providing explanations, presenting an argument and producing a work which attempts to follow assessment criteria. The essay also fits comfortably into this genre by adhering to some of the structural and linguistic conventions typically found in traditional student essays. For example, even though much of the text is spoken, the essay uses the semi-formal register of academic essay writing. It also cites the sources of its ideas and in some cases quotes directly from sources as one would expect to find in academic writing; however, in some instances, this use of other sources, unlike a traditional student essay, is displayed with an embedded video clip of the scholar speaking directly to an audience. At the end of this digital essay is a typewritten list of sources, akin to the reference page which concludes a traditional essay. The essay's introduction also follows the textual convention of giving an overview of topics covered, though it does so with words across a screen while an image in the background shows the evolutionary process of life on earth in eclipsed time lapses. This mixing of modes (the televisual and the written) with their own independent meanings could be interpreted together as a metaphor or as saying that digital essays and digital learning are undergoing an evolutionary process at high speed. A second part of the introduction takes place with Murray on the screen introducing himself and talking about the purpose of the assignment.

The features which make Murray's essay belong to a hybrid genre are many. The example just given of a two-part introduction, opening with an entertaining video clip already shows a departure from traditional essay-writing structures. Table 8.1 summarises this hybridity with examples, their generic type and the intertextual references employed (Table 8.1).

As the table illustrates, many genres have been combined in this student essay. This illustrates not only its hybridity and use of intertextuality and interdiscursivity, but the ways in which it uses some of the affordances of digital technologies, which encourages the mixing of genres. A further analysis of this essay could draw from Bakhtin's concept of **dialogism**, which highlights the ways this work engages with previous texts, as well as how the text anticipates readers' reactions.

TABLE 8.1 HYBRIDITY EXAMPLES FROM A DIGITAL ESSAY

Hybridity Examples from a Digital Essay (Murray, 2009)

Essay text	Genre type	Intertextual reference
Opening credits and sequence: a film clip about evolution	Entertainment/education film	'Push the Tempo' by Fat Boy Slim
Written text of a Course Description	Higher education course descriptions	Course Description for the MA in E-Learning and Digital Culture, University of Edinburgh
'Andy's E-Learning and Digital Cultures Blog'	Blog set in a VLE, with various genres within	Student's original blog
Video clip of a teacher describing how to write an essay	Classroom instruction	Teaching video clip (source unknown)
A quote in written mode: 'a move from the fixed to the fluid, the text is no longer contained between the coves or by the limits of the page'	Academic PowerPoint slide, and written essay	Merchant 2007
Video clip of a public talk by Dr Patrick Dixon talking about digital communication and plagiarism	Public talk in a conference environment	Globalchange.com
Video clip of Dr Henry Jenkins talking about the new media systems and changes to our culture	Documentary	(source unknown)
Scene from *Metropolis* with text across the screen from the original silent film and from Murray's essay	Entertainment: silent film; and student essay	*Metropolis* (1927) Fritz Lang
A postscript to the essay: embedded story set with fictional characters played by actors	Situation comedy	(source unknown)

While the engagement with some texts is for academic purposes, other texts are engaged with in humorous ways with the intention of entertaining readers.

Superdiversity

Here we will look at the concept of **superdiversity** as it has been applied to language by Blommaert and Rampton (2011) to account for certain features found in online language which have emerged from the international audiences afforded to writers on the internet. As its name suggests, superdiversity refers to the multiculturalism which has sprung up in recent decades across the world as a result of immigration, globalisation of businesses and industry and the ease of international communication and travel. When applied to language use, it accounts for elements in texts which show traces of this cultural and linguistic diversity. The growing interest among scholars to examine language and superdiversity follows on from research in multilingualism along with the influence of Mikhail Bakhtin's work. Bakhtin's concept of **heteroglossia** has brought attention to the way language production by individuals comes from reusing the expressions and styles of others. Throughout this book we have seen examples of digital text and digital talk which display heteroglossia; here we add to our analyses of such texts the concept of superdiversity.

Along with heteroglossia, other terms have been used in linguistics to describe aspects of superdiversity, such as code-switching, code-mixing and style-shifting. Code-switching refers to instances where speakers switch between languages or language varieties during a conversation and is a term mainly used to describe speech. Code-mixing is a similar concept, but while code-switching refers to any stretch of speech, from an individual lexeme to a string of utterances, code-mixing accounts for switching within a sentence from one language or language variety to another. Both of these terms have been used mainly in research of conversational discourse, but nonetheless display cross-cultural and linguistic diversity. The term style-shifting differs from code-switching and code-mixing in that it is mainly used to describe switching between styles of discourse within a language or language variety; for example, a speaker might have one style of speech when speaking to an adult, but a very different style when speaking to a child, and this switch might occur within the same conversation. A related concept worth considering is language-crossing; this occurs when a speaker of one language or variety of language knowingly adopts another language or variety of language which are marked in their use as not belonging to that speaker. When exploring superdiversity in online communication, whether digital text or digital talk, all of these concepts come into play.

Consider the example below of a comment to a Facebook upload of a YouTube clip which used Singlish, a Singaporean variety of English (ellipses in the original):

> Wow … ayoh … U two really Boleh Tahan! Another good one … make me laughing bodoh

By the author's own admission, this comment is an English speaker's attempt at writing in Singlish. In other words, this is an example of language-crossing, as well as superdiversity. There is enough Singlish in the comment to see that it functions as part of the discourse community which includes people who follow Boleh Tahan's YouTube videos, as well as for those who recognise Singlish.

In the example tweet below, Hindustani is mixed with English and a couple of emoticons:

> Kuch bhi karneka lekin #ego ko hurt nahi karneka ☹ but some people are born to do just that ☺

The translation of the first part of this tweet is 'whatever you do don't hurt my ego'. This particular example could be treated as code-mixing aimed at readers of Hindustani and English. With knowledge of only one of the two languages, the Hindustani portion makes sense on its own, but the use of emoticons might be unclear without an understanding of English. The English portion, however, does not make sense on its own without knowing the reference for the referent 'that'.

Other examples of superdiversity can be found in cross-cultural styles of communication. In Chapter 3 we referred to one such example, the study by DeAndrea, Shaw and Levine (2010), where Asian users of Facebook exhibited a communication style characteristic of non-Asian users of the SNS. We also saw in Chapter 3 a Facebook status update where the author self-mockingly tried to reproduce a Southern American accent, a language variety different from his own.

While the examples given here pertain to the written mode in online communication, superdiversity could just as easily be applied to multimodal communication, which, as we have noted, is abundant in digital textuality. Writing about language and superdiversity, Blommaert and Rampton (2011) make this salient point:

> [...] with people communicating more and more in varying combinations of oral, written, pictorial and 'design' modes (going on Facebook, playing online games, using mobile phones, etc.), multimodal analysis is an inevitable empirical adjustment to contemporary conditions [...] (p. 6)

The Buddha Smiled

In Chapter 1 we used this interesting blog to illustrate deictic reference and hyperlinking as found in digital texts; here we revisit this blog as an example of both genre hybridity and superdiversity. The Buddha Smiled is a personal blog and, typical of such texts, it generally adheres to the genre of journal entries and autobiography. Like many blogs, it also mixes genres by linking to other texts, such as online news articles, and embedding other genres through intertextuality and the blogger's own works, including fictional prose. Throughout this fascinating blog, examples of superdiversity can be found.

The profile of The Buddha Smiled refers to the blogger in the third person, breaking from the convention of keeping the profile a first-person summary, which would follow the first-person autobiographical style of most blogs. The profile on the blogging homepage reads as follows (a longer version of this profile is available via a hyperlink):

> The Buddha Smiled is a world citizen with a distinctly Indian flavour. Thanks to daddy ji's job, he grew up in 4 different continents, went to 10 different schools, and speaks about 6 different languages (2 fluently, 2 reasonably well, and 1 appallingly – apparently his accent is that of a Colombian hooker asking for money after a job). He also has a fictitious Polish grandmother, Ida Rosenberg. Having worked in banking in the City of London for four years, he finally had enough in March 2009 when he managed to get out with his soul intact, but with highly irregular sleeping patterns and a terrible spending habit.

Superdiversity is marked linguistically in the use of '*ji*' which in Hindi is an honorific. This profile prepares the reader for the blog with its cross-cultural references and marked examples of linguistic superdiversity. In addition, this profile anticipates the genre hybridity which occurs in the blog, mixing non-fiction with fiction, in the form of a 'fictitious grandmother'.

Other languages appear in this blog without translation into English. After describing the music he is listening to, The Buddha Smiled gives readers the lyrics to the French song '*As-tu déjà aimé?*' by Alex Beaupain. This instance of intertextuality and code-switching can be interpreted in different ways; it could be to bond with French speakers, perhaps to the exclusion of others, or it could be to display the superdiversity of the blogger's world, as part of his self-presentation. Similarly, another day's blog includes references to Indian food (such as *mooli parathas, chai and masala dosa*) in the context of a typical Sunday in Britain. Here too, translations and explanations are absent.

Included in the blog are many film reviews, which take on some of the generic conventions of language and style found in reviews in newsprint and online news sites. We can see this in the example review below of a Bollywood film:

> Sadly, while King Khan does his best to emulate a *paan* chewing rustic from the Gangetic plains, high on *bhaang* and also on the *tambaaku* in his *beeda*, this is where you miss the old Bachchan.

The blog also displays an awareness of an international audience by explaining the occasional reference from Indian history and culture. For example, one of his posts about a Delhi marathon is entitled '*Ab Dilli Door Nahnin*', which is explained at the end of the posting as a reference to the 1847 War of Independence. At the same time, there is also religious superdiversity throughout with references to Buddhism and Hinduism, which an international audience is likely to understand.

Activity

Visit one or two of the EFL teacher blogs listed below and consider these blogs in terms of superdiversity. Do you find examples of

> code-mixing or style-shifting which mark different languages and cultures?
>
> http://idleeflthoughts.wordpress.com/
>
> http://teflbloggers.com/day-3-beijing/
>
> http://tefltecher.wordpress.com/

Conclusions

We started this book by defining digital texts and digital talk and setting out ways to analyse digital textuality using different approaches and mapping these approaches to each other where appropriate. For much of this book, we have used social semiotics, both in the form of Halliday's Systemic Functional Linguistics and multimodal analysis from the work of Kress and van Leeuwen. These approaches have been used in tandem with Conversational Analysis and Discourse Analysis for digital talk and with Text World Theory for digital texts and talk involving fiction writing. We have also drawn upon concepts and frameworks used in linguistics for analysing certain types of writing; we have employed terms found in literary stylistics in order to describe features of language used in digital poetry, and have considered the approaches of Bell and Critical Discourse Analysis in looking at the conventions and language uses found in news writing. In this final chapter we have added a layer to the analyses offered by looking at genre hybridity and superdiversity as these concepts relate to digital textuality.

While genre hybridity and superdiversity exist off-line in printed and face-to-face communication, digital technologies and the world-wide extent of digital communication make these features more abundant. Consider for example the SNS features of comments and 'likes' appearing in other genres, such as news sites and the Urban Dictionary. These features are part of the platforms given to these sites by their designers, encouraging genre hybridity. In other cases, such as advertisements appearing in Twitter, while the technology of microblogging does not necessarily encourage advertising, the potential for large audiences through retweets and followers of followers brings about this hybridity.

We also need to recognise new genres which have emerged with digital technologies and their impact on current linguistic theories on language. Writing in 2013, Herring commented that 'there are new types of content to be analysed: status updates, text annotations on video, tags on social bookmarking sites, and edits on wikis' (p. 5). In this book, we have set out to provide the groundwork for approaching these new types of content, drawing on existing theories. For example, in Chapter 3 we looked at social bookmarking sites and the variety of linguistic conventions in tagging. In Chapter 3 we also analysed status updates in some SNSs for their language features and for the ways in which they expressed identity through self-presentation. In Chapter 2 we considered the edits on wikis, applying Halliday's meanings of language to articulate how these edits relate to the main texts. Further research and analyses of these new forms of texts are needed and could bring about new models for looking at language.

Scholars have also noted the need for linguistic analysis to consider how contexts are changing, such as SNSs with local versions in different languages. Moreover, technologies are changing in ways which go beyond computers; as mentioned earlier, mobile phones provide unique platforms for SNSs. Televisions are also beginning to act more like computers, with interactive communication possible through TV-mediated text messaging (text messaging through a television screen, while watching programmes); this adds to the social context of computing as it moves from what is for the most part solidary interaction with a screen to group interaction.

Many of the examples of genre hybridity discussed so far can be treated as the merging of texts into one text type, but where the two separate texts are visible or distinguishable. For example, news articles which are directly followed by comments could be treated as one text with two discourse genres. Presumably, but not always, these discourses have the same or closely related fields. In some cases the news articles and the comments might share aspects of the tenor, such as register, though in other cases the interpersonal meanings of these two text types might be different. For example, a news article critical of the police might have a comment from someone identifying themselves as connected with the police; that is, the comment is meant to be seen as coming from an authority, someone with inside knowledge of the situation described in the article.

To conclude, an overview of this book would be right to portray it as describing and analysing changes to writing practices, as writing is a mode used in both digital texts and digital talk. Glazier (2008) makes the pertinent point that 'the digital text signals not only a change in writing practices but part of a change in the consciousness of the entire culture' (p. 28).

Sample projects

1. Create a table to compare the occurrence of generic linguistic and textual features of traditional student essays, which you can find in the two digital essays listed below:
   a. http://www.teachthought.com/technology/21-creative-digital-essays-that-you-can-use-in-your-classroom/
   b. http://prezi.com/1qbpbuquqbvs/heart-of-darkness-digital-essay/
2. Using the same two digital essays from Sample Project 1 above, create a table where you list other genres found within each essay, following the format of Table 8.1. Consider the hybridity, intertextuality and interdiscursivity of each genre you identify.

Further reading

Bhatia, V. (2004) *Worlds of Written Discourse: A Genre-Based View*. London: Continuum.

Building on Halliday's work, this book provides a clear and comprehensive guide to genre, along with discussions of examples and the development of genre approaches over the years.

Diversities (2011). vol. 13, no. 2, available at http://www.unesco.org/shs/diversities/vol13/issue2/

This issue of the *Diversities* journal is entitled 'Language and Superdiversities' and focuses on this subject with five articles. Of particular relevance to the ideas discussed in this chapter are: Blommaert, J. and Rampton, B. 'Language and Superdiversity', and Varis, P. and Wang, X. 'Superdiversity on the Internet: a case from China'.

Fairclough, N., Cortese, G, and Ardizzone, P. (2007) *Discourse and Contemporary Social Change*. Bern, Switzerland: Peter Lang.

Relevant to both genre hybridity and superdiversity, this collection of articles draws from research in discourse analysis to examine how discourses emerge and develop at times of social change.

Websites used in this chapter

The Buddha Smiled (http://thebuddhasmiled.blogspot.co.uk/)

Urban Dictionary (http://www.urbandictionary.com/)

Murray, D. (2009) Digital Essay (http://vimeo.com/8278368)

Glossary

adjacency pairs   A two-part exchange in conversation where the second utterance is functionally dependent on the first. For example, Speaker A says 'Thank you', and Speaker B replies 'You're welcome'.

coherence   Related to the term **cohesion**. The property which texts have when they are said to make sense and have unity. In SFL, coherence is related to textual meanings of language.

cohesion   The interconnectedness between sentences in a text. There are two types of cohesion, grammatical and lexical. Grammatical accounts for the use of connecting words, such as conjunctions, and referencing words, such as pronouns and demonstrative adjectives; lexical cohesion refers to links made through sense relations, such as **synonymy** and **hyponymy**. Cohesion is often used with the related concept of **coherence**, and they can be difficult to distinguish when applying them to texts. In SFL, like coherence, cohesion is related to textual meanings of language.

conceptual pattern   From multimodal semiotics, this refers to the visual representation of participants' generalised characteristics, such as class, age and social significance found in images.

deixis   From the Greek for 'pointing' or 'showing'. The property of language which some words have to orientate the speaker/writer in the context of space and time. For example, demonstrative adjectives such as *here*, *there*, *this* and *that* orientate the speaker/writer's proximity in space; adverbs such as *now* and *then* orientate the speaker/writer's proximity in time.

dialogism   (also referred to as *dialogicality*) From the works of Mikhail Bakhtin, this refers to the way all utterances are in response to what has been said before and in anticipation to what will be said.

discourse world In TWT, the background knowledge, such as cultural context, and the knowledge of the given text shared between writer and reader.

face work In sociology and sociolinguistics 'face' refers to our positively valued social identities, and face work is how we manage these identities for ourselves and others. For example, we might act or speak in a way as to save face.

field In SFL, this is an element of **ideational meaning**, which accounts for what the text is about (i.e., its meaningful content).

foregrounding The way in which some language and images in a given context become perceptually noticeable or prominent.

function-advancing propositions In TWT, these propositions account for the states, actions and processes which move a story forward.

genre This term has two related meanings: 1) to refer to text types, such as fictional prose and poetry; 2) to refer to a communicative event, distinguished by other events by its purpose. Both senses are used in this book and drawn together in a discussion in Chapter 8.

Grice's Maxims A subset of Grice's cooperative principle, which stipulates that there is a shared assumption by the participants in a conversation that they will cooperate with each other for the purpose of their conversation by keeping to conventional maxims. These maxims are: Quality, say that which you believe to be true; Quantity, provide enough information for the conversation; Relation, be relevant; and Manner, be precise and clear.

heteroglossia From the Greek meaning 'many voices', a term coined by Mikhail Bakhtin. Accounts for the way discourse is made up of voices and texts associated with different contexts. This covers a range of borrowings from intertextual references of specific texts to using phrases which carry a sense of coming from another source.

hyponymy The relationship between terms in which one term is superordinate to another. For example, a dog is a hyponym of animal, with animal the superordinate term.

ideational meaning In SFL, the metafunction of language which relates to the message and experience of communication. The main element of ideational meaning is the **field**.

interpersonal meaning In SFL, the metafunction of language which relates to the construction of relationships between speaker/listener or writer/reader. The main element of interpersonal meaning is the **tenor**.

intertextuality   The way in which texts borrow or incorporate other texts. The use of this term ranges from a broad scope, which would include genre, as it involves the use of styles and conventions of other texts, to a narrower direct reference to other specific texts.

Jakobson's functions of language   Jakobson proposed six functions of language: Referential, Emotive, Conative, Phatic, Metalingual and Poetic Functions. In this book we make reference to the Emotive Function, which is oriented on the addresser and focuses on the expressing of emotions (as opposed to giving information); and the Poetic Function, which is oriented on the text and focuses on the message for its own sake, that is, the way something is expressed.

Labov's elements of oral narratives   Labov described narratives as containing six elements: the abstract (a summary of the story); the orientation (referring to background information for the story, such as the place, time and people involved); complicating actions (the happenings of the story); the evaluation (can occur at different points throughout the story and justifies its telling); the resolution (the ending of the story); and the coda (the point where the story telling ends and the narrator signals its ending by bringing the listener back into the present time and place).

lexia   In digital texts, these are nodes or small texts which are the destination texts of hyperlinks.

lexical density   The proportion of lexical items (such as nouns, verbs, adverbs and adjectives) to grammatical items (pronouns, conjunctions and prepositions). Where the proportion of lexical items are higher than grammatical items, for example in written textbooks, they are said to have a higher lexical density.

linearity   A property pertaining to a step-by-step logic. When referring to narrative, it refers to ways elements of story-telling have identifiable beginnings, middles and endings and are brought together into a coherent whole.

literacy practices   The ways people interact with texts, which includes the reading of texts and conversation around texts.

metonymy   The relationship between words in which one word is substituted for another with which it has a close association. For example, the White House to represent the US President and people who work for the President.

modality   The expression of a speaker/writer's attitude or stance towards what they are saying. This could be, for example, in relation to its truth (epistemic modality) or in relation to its likelihood (deontic modality). In SFL, modality is related to interpersonal meanings of language.

modal world In TWT, this depicts the internal worlds of narrators and characters. In line with the concept of **modality** there are basically three modal worlds: 1) boulomaic modal worlds, which represent desires; 2) deontic modal worlds, which relate to obligations; and 3) epistemic modal worlds, which depict hypothetical worlds, or possible worlds.

mode In SFL, an element of the **textual meaning** of language; this accounts for the way in which communication is transmitted, such as written or spoken words and images.

multimodality The property which texts have to contain more than one mode, for example, written language with images.

parallelism A type of **foregrounding** in which some features, such as grammatical structure or sound, remain constant through repetition. For example, 'Like father, like son', which repeats the grammatical structure with the two clauses and which also repeats the word 'like'.

polysemy The ability of single lexemes to have multiple meanings. For example, *pupil* can refer to a part of the eye or it can refer to a student.

presentational pattern From multimodal semiotics this refers to the participants found in images as belonging to or enacting a narrative.

register A variety of a language used for a particular purpose in a particular social context, including the use of formal or informal language. In SFL, register is related to interpersonal meanings of language and the element of **tenor**.

superdiversity The presence of multiculturalism; in this book this is placed in the context of language use and is discussed more fully in Chapter 8.

synonymy The relationship between two lexemes, whereby they share the same sense. Many words in English can be said to be near-synonyms, for example, 'simple' and 'plain'.

tenor In SFL, an element of the **interpersonal meaning** of language; this accounts for social roles and relationships between participants in communication. Included in tenor is the **register** of the text.

textual meaning In SFL, the metafunction of language which relates to the organisation and presentation of texts and includes **cohesion**, **coherence** and **tenor**.

text world   In TWT, this refers to the world created by a text, which as a text develops forms part of the **discourse world** shared between writer and reader.

transitivity   Not to be confused with a type of verb which takes an object in traditional grammars, transitivity analysis, which is referred to in this book, derives from SFL. It describes experiences expressed in language as containing three basic elements or process structures; these are: the process itself, the participants in the process, and the circumstances surrounding the process. Halliday distinguishes six process types. The four main process types, which we use in this book, are: material (which involves doing), mental (which involves experiencing or sensing), verbal (which involves saying or writing) and relational (which involves classifying and identifying). Participants can be described as actors and goals, along with other more specific terms, such as 'sensor' and 'sayer'. In SFL, transitivity analysis helps us to explore **ideational meanings**.

world-building elements   In TWT, these elements account for the sense of time and place along with the objects and characters of the text.

Bibliography

Allen, S. (2006) *Online News*. Maidenhead: Open University Press.
Amerika, M. (2007) *Meta/data: A Digital Poetics*. Cambridge, MA: MIT Press.
Andrews, J. (1997) 'Seattle Drift', http://www.vispo.com/animisms/SeattleDrift. html#, date accessed 10 June 2013.
Andrews, R. and Haythornthwaite, C. (eds) (2007) *The SAGE Handbook of E-Learning Research*. London: Sage Publications.
Androutsopoulos, J. (2006) 'Introduction: Sociolinguistics and Computer-Mediated Communication'. *Journal of Sociolinguistics*, 10(4), pp. 419–438.
Amrhein, S. 'Demolition Begins at Home Where Sinkhole Swallowed Florida Man', 3 March. http://articles. Chicagotribune.com, date accessed 4 March 2013.
Aarseth, E.J. (1997) *Cybertext: Perspectives on Ergodic Literature*. Baltimore: The Johns Hopkins University Press.
Azariah, D.R. (2012) 'Beyond the Blog: The Networked Self of Travel Bloggers on Twitter', *Platform: Journal of Media and Communication*, 4(1). http://journals. culture-communication, date accessed 2 February 2013.
Abu Bakar, N. (2009) 'E-Learning Environment: Blogging as a Platform for Language Learning', *European Journal of Social Sciences*, 9(4), pp. 594–604.
Bakhtin, M.M. (1981) *The Dialogic Imagination: Four Essays*. USA: University of Texas Press.
Barr, M. and Barton, K. (2008) 'How My Brain Betrays Me', YouTube. http://www.youtube.com/watch?v=xUfMgbknvnQ, date accessed 12 February 2013.
Barthes, R. (1974) *S/Z*. London: Cape Books.
Barton, D. (2010) 'Vernacular Writing on the Web', in *The Anthropology of Writing: Understanding Textually-Mediated Worlds*, pp. 112–125. London: Continuum.
Barton, D. and Lee, C. (2013) *Language Online: Investigating Digital Texts and Practices*. 1st ed. Abingdon: Routledge.
Baym, N.K. (2010) *Personal Connections in the Digital Age*. London: Polity.
Bell, A. (1991) *The Language of News Media*. Oxford: Blackwell.
Bell, A. (2010) *The Possible Worlds of Hypertext Fiction*. Basingstoke: Palgrave Macmillan.

Bell, A, Astrid, E. and Rustad, H (eds) (2013) *Analyzing Digital Fiction*. London: Routledge.
Bennet, S., Maton, K. and Kervin, L. (2008) 'The "Digital Natives" Debate: A Critical Review of the Evidence', *British Journal of Educational Technology*, 39(5), pp. 775–786.
Bezemer, J. and Kress, G. (2008) 'Writing in Multimodal Texts A Social Semiotic Account of Designs for Learning', *Written Communication*, 25(2), pp. 166–195.
Bhatia, V. (2004) *Worlds of Written Discourse: A Genre-Based View*. London: Continuum International Publishing Group.
Blommaert, J and Rampton, B. (2011) 'Language and Superdiversity', *Diversities*, 13(2). www.unesco.org/shs/diversities/vol13/issue2/art1, date accessed 10 July 2013.
Boczkowski, P.J. (2005) *Digitizing the News: Innovation in Online Newspapers*. Massachusetts: MIT Press.
Bolter, J.D. (2001) *Writing Space: Computers, Hypertext, and the Remediation of Print*. New York: Routledge.
Boyd, D. and Ellison, N. (2007) 'Social Network Sites: Definition, History, and Scholarship', *Journal of Computer-Mediated Communication*, 13(1). http://jcmc.indiana.edu/vol13/issue1/, date accessed 7 February 2013.
Busbee, J. (2013) 'Oscar Pistorius Nike Ad Takes on New, Chilling Resonance after Tragedy'. *Yahoo Sports*. http://sports.yahoo.com/blogs/, 14 February, date accessed 15 February, 2013.
Brown, G. and Yule, G. (1983) *Discourse Analysis*. Cambridge: Cambridge University Press.
Butt, D., Fahey, R., Feez, S. and Yallop, C. (2001) *Using Functional Grammar: An Explorer's Guide,* 2nd ed. Sydney: National Centre for English Language Teaching and Research, Macquarie University.
Caldas-Coulthard, C.R, and Toolan, M.J. (eds). (2005) *The Writer's Craft, the Culture's Technology PALA 2002*. Amsterdam; New York: Rodopi.
Carr, C.T., Schrock, D.B. and Dauterman, P. (2012) 'Speech Acts Within Facebook Status Messages', *Journal of Language and Social Psychology*, 31(2), pp. 176–196.
Clark, U. (2007) *Studying Language: English in Action*. Basingstoke: Palgrave Macmillan.
Conboy, M. (2007) *The Language of the News*. London: Routledge.
Crum, A. (2013) 'Florida Sinkhole Opens Up, Swallows Man', *WebProNews*, 1 March. http://www.webpronews.com/, date accessed 15 March 2013.
Crystal, D. (2001) *Language and the Internet*. Cambridge, UK; New York: Cambridge University Press.
Crystal, D. (2004) *A Glossary of Netspeak and Textspeak*. Edinburgh: Edinburgh University Press.
DeAndrea, D.C., Shaw, A.S. and Levine, T.R. (2010) 'Online Language: The Role of Culture in Self-Expression and Self-Construal on Facebook'. *Journal of Language and Social Psychology*, 29(4), pp. 425–442.
Dillon, G.L. (2005) 'Anti-Loakoon: Mixed and Merged Modes of Imagetext on the Web', in C.R. Caldas-Coulthard. and M.J. Toolan (eds) *The Writer's Craft, The Culture's Technology*. Amsterdam; New York: Rodopi, pp. 1–22.

Doudaki, V. and Spyridou, L.-P. (2012) 'Print and Online News', *Journalism Studies*, 14(6), pp. 1–19.
Douglas, J.Y. (2001) *The End of Books – Or Books Without End? Reading Interactive Narratives*. Ann Arbor: University of Michigan Press.
Engelbrecht Fisher, C. (2013) 'I'm a Victim of Gun Violence. I'm Also a Video Game Developer', http://www.slate.com/blogs/, date accessed 1 March 2013.
Ensslin, A. (2007) *Canonizing Hypertext: Explorations and Constructions*. London: Continuum.
Ensslin, A. (2012) '"I want to Say I may have Seen my Son die this Morning": Unintentional Unreliable Narration in Digital Fiction'. *Language and Literature*, 21(2), pp. 136–149.
Fairclough, N. (1992) *Discourse and Social Change*. Cambridge: Polity Press.
Fairclough, N. (2001) *Language and Power* (2nd ed). Harlow: Pearson.
Fairclough, N., Cortese, G. and Ardizzone, P. (2007) *Discourse and Contemporary Social Change*. Bern, Switzerland: Peter Lang.
Feng, J. (2012) 'Have Mouse, Will Travel'. In: *From Codex to Hypertext: Reading at the Turn of the Twenty-first Century*. pp. 48–68.
Firth, J.R. (1957) *Papers in Linguistics, 1934–1951*. London: Oxford University Press.
Fowler, R. (1991) *Language in the News: Discourse and Ideology in the Press*. London: Routledge.
Fullwood, C., Morris, N. and Evans, L. (2011) 'Linguistic Androgyny on MySpace'. *Journal of Language and Social Psychology*, 30(1), pp. 114–124.
Funkhouser, C.T. (2012) *New Directions in Digital Poetry: 1*. London: Continuum.
Garfinkel, H. (1967) *Studies in Ethnomethodology*. Englewood Cliffs, NJ: Prentice Hall.
Gavins, J (2000), 'Absurd Tricks with Bicycle Frames in the Text World of the Third Policeman', Nottingham Linguistic Circular 15: 17–33.
Gavins, J. (2007) *Text World Theory: An Introduction*. Edinburgh: Edinburgh University Press.
Gavins, J. and Steen, G. (2003) *Cognitive Poetics in Practice*. London: Routledge.
Gibbons, A. (2012) *Multimodality, Cognition and Experimental Literature*. London: Routledge.
Gilster, P. (1998) *Digital Literacy*. New York; Chichester: Wiley Computer.
Glazier, L.P. (2008) *Digital Poetics: The Making of E-Poetries*. 1st ed. Tuscaloosa, Alabama: University Alabama Press.
Goffman, E. (1959) *The Presentation of the Self in Everyday Life*. Garden City, NY: Doubleday.
Goffman, E. (1981) *Forms of Talk*. Philadelphia: University of Pennsylvania Press.
Goodman S. et al. (eds) (2003) *Language, Literacy and Education: A Reader*. Staffordshire: Trentham Books.
Gunter, B., Campbell, V., Touri, M. and Gibson, R. (2009) 'Blogs, News and Credibility', *Aslib Proceedings*, 61(2), pp. 185–204.
Halliday, M.A.K. (1978) *Language as Social Semiotic*, London: Edward Arnold.

Halliday, M. and Matthiessen, C. (2004) *An Introduction to Functional Grammar*. 3rd ed. London and New York: Hodder Education.

Hayles, N.K. (2000) 'Flickering Connectivities in Shelley Jackson's Patchwork Girl : The Importance of Media-Specific Analysis', *Postmodern Culture*, 10(2). http://muse.jhu.edu /journals/postmodern_culture/, date accessed 29 April 2013.

Hayles, N.K. (2008) *Electronic Literature: New Horizons for the Literary*. Notre Dame, IN: University of Notre Dame.

Heintz, J and Karmanau, Y. (2013) 'Statue of Lenin Torn Down in Kiev amid Huge Pro-EU Protest'. 8 December, http://www.independent.co.uk, date accessed 10 December 2013.

Herring, S.C., Scheidt, L.A., Wright, E. and Bonus, S. (2005) 'Weblogs as a Bridging Genre', *Information Technology & People*, 18(2), pp. 142–171.

Herring, S.C. (2013) 'Discourse in Web 2.0: Familiar, Reconfigured and Emergent'. In: Tannen, D. and Trester, A.M. (eds) *Discourse 2.0: Language and New Media*. Washington, DC: Georgetown University Press.

Institute of Creative Technologies of De Montfort University (2008) *A Million Penguins Research Report,* http://www.amillionpenguins.com/, date accessed 28 July 2013.

Jackson, S. (1995) *Patchwork Girl*. Watertown, MA: Eastgate Systems.

Jakobson, R. (1960) 'Closing Statement, Linguistics and Poetics', in T. Sebeok (ed) *Style in Language*. Cambridge, MA: MIT Press.

Jewitt, C. (2008) 'Multimodality and Literacy in School Classrooms'. *Review of Research in Education*, 32(1), pp. 241–267.

Johnstone, B. (2008) *Discourse Analysis*. Oxford: Blackwell.

Joyce, M. (1996) *Twelve Blue*. http://www.eastgate.com/TwelveBlue/, date accessed 9 April 2013.

Kac. E. (ed) (2007) *Media Poetics: An International Anthology*. Bristol: Intellect.

Kress, G.R. and van Leeuwen, T. (2006) *Reading Images: The Grammar of Visual Design*. London: Routledge.

Labov, W. and Waletzky, J. (1967) 'Narrative Analysis: Oral Versions of Personal Narratives', in *Essays on the Verbal and Visual Arts*. Seattle: University of Washington Press.

Landow, G.P. (2006) *Hypertext 3.0: Critical Theory and New Media in an Era of Globalization*. Baltimore: JHU Press.

Lasica, J.D. (2003) 'Blogs and Journalism Need Each Other', J.D. Lasica, http://www.jdlasica.com, date accessed 3 March 2003.

Liu, H., Maes, P. and Davenport, G. (2006) 'Unraveling the Taste Fabric of Social Networks,' *International Journal of Semantic Web and Information Systems*. Vol. 2, No. 1, pp. 42–71.

Malinowski, B. (1923) 'The Problem of Meaning in Primitive Languages'. In: C.K. Ogden and I.A. Richards (eds) *The Meaning of Meaning*. London: Routledge, pp. 296–336.

Martin, A. (2009) 'Digital Literacy in the Third Age: Sustaining Identity in an Uncertain World'. *e-learning papers*, 12 http://www.elearningeuropa.eu, date accessed 10 December 2013.

Martin, J.R. (1984) *Language, Register, Genre*. London: Routledge.

Mathes, A. (2004) 'Folksonomies: Cooperative Classification and Communication through Shared Media,' *Computer Mediated Communication*, December. [http://www.adammathes.com/academic/computer-mediated-communication/folksonomies.html] Last accessed 17 July 2014.

Maynard, N. (2001) 'Digitalisation and the News' Neiman Reports'. Winter 12–13.

Meredith S. and Newton, B. (2004). 'Models of e-learning: a comparative case study', *International Journal of Management Education*. Vol. 1, No. 1.

Miles, A. (2002) 'Hypertext Structure as the Event of Connection', *Journal of Digital Information*, 2. http://journals.tdl.org/jodi/article/view/48, date accessed 28 June 2012.

Morris, A.K. and Swiss, T. (eds) (2009) *New Media Poetics: Contexts, Technotexts, and Theories*. Cambridge, Mass.; London: MIT Press.

Murray, D. (2009) Digital Essay, http://vimeo.com/8278368, date accessed 19 November 2013.

Myers, G. (2010) *The Discourse of Blogs and Wikis*. London: Continuum International Publishing Group.

Nelson, J. (2010) 'Sydney's Siberia', http://www.secrettechnology.com/sydney/sibera.html, date accessed 10 March 2013.

Page, R.E. (2011) *Stories and Social Media: Identities and Interaction*. London: Routledge.

Pullinger, K. and Joseph, C. (no date) *Flight Paths*. http://www.flightpaths.net/, date accessed 26 August 2013.

Prensky, M. (2001) 'Digital Natives, Digital Immigrants', *On the Horizon*, 9(5), pp. 1–6.

Rettberg, S. (2011) 'All Together Now: Hypertext, Collective Narratives and Online Collective Knowledge Communities', in R. Page and B. Thomas (eds) *New Narratives: Stories and Storytelling in the Digital Age*. Lincoln, NE: University of Nebraska.

Robinson, S. (2006) 'The Mission of the j-blog Recapturing Journalistic Authority Online'. *Journalism*, 7(1), pp. 65–83.

Ryan, M.L. (2001) *Narrative As Virtual Reality: Immersion and Interactivity in Literature and Electronic Media*. Baltimore: J. Hopkins University Press.

Sacks, H. (1992) *Lectures on Conversation* (ed., by Gail Jefferson). Oxford: Blackwell.

Schneider, R. (2005) 'Hypertext Narrative and the Reader: A View from Cognitive Theory'. *European Journal of English Studies*, 9(2), pp. 197–208.

Schäfer, J. and Gendolla, P. (eds) (2010) *Beyond the Screen: Transformations of Literary Structures, Interfaces and Genres*. Germany: Transcript Verlag.

Seargeant, P. and Tagg, C. (2014) *The Language of Social Media: Identity and Community on the Internet*. Basingstoke: Palgrave Macmillan

Semino, E. (2002) 'A Cognitive Stylistics Approach to Mind Style in Narrative Fiction'. In: Semino, E. and Culpeper, J. (eds) *Cognitive Stylistics: Language and Cognition in Text Analysis*, pp. 95–122. London: John Benjamin.

Short, M. (1996) *Exploring the Language of Poems, Plays and Prose*. Harlow: Pearson Education.

Sinclair, J. and Coulthard, M. (1975) *Towards an Analysis of Discourse: The English Used by Teachers and Pupils.* Oxford: OUP.

Snyder, I. (ed) (2002) *Silicon Literacies: Communication, Innovation and Education in the Electronic Age.* London: Routledge.

Stephens, P. (2004) 'Samantha in Winter', http://www.paulspages.co.uk/htext/saminwinter.htm, date accessed 9 Aug. 2012.

Stockwell, P. (2002) *Cognitive Poetics: An Introduction.* London: Routledge.

Stockwell, P. (2003) 'Surreal Figures'. In: Gavins, J. and G. Steen (eds) *Cognitive Poetics in Practice.* London: Routledge.

Swales, J.M. (1990) *Genre Analysis: English in Academic and Research Settings.* Cambridge: Cambridge University Press.

Tagg, C. (2012) 'Digital English', in D. Allington and B. Mayor (eds) *Communicating in English: Talk Text, Technology*, pp. 307–335. London: Routledge.

Tannen, D. and Trester, A.M. (eds) (2013) *Discourse 2.0: Language and New Media.* Washington: Georgetown University Press.

The Buddha Smiled, thebuddhasmiled.blogspot.co.uk, date accessed 22 November 2013.

Thurlow, C., Lengel, L.B. and Tomic, A. (2004) *Computer Mediated Communication: Social Interaction and the Internet.* London: Sage.

Treanor, J. (2013) 'Barclays and RBS paid 523 Staff more than £1m a Year', *The Guardian.* 8 March, http://www.guardian.co.uk/, date accessed 9 March 2013.

Tremayne, M., Zheng, N., Lee, J.K. and Jeong, J. (2006) 'Issue Publics on the Web: Applying Network Theory to the War Blogosphere', *Journal of Computer-Mediated Communication*, 12, pp. 290–310.

Trimarco, P. (2012a) 'Stylistic Approaches to Teaching Hypertext Fiction'. In: Burke, M., S. Csabi, L. Week and J. Zerkowitz (eds) *Pedagogical Stylistics: Current Trends in Language, Literature and ELT*, London: Continuum.

Trimarco, P. (2012b) 'Employing Pragmatic Stylistics: A Case Study of Students' Online Discussions', *European Journal of Applied Linguistics and TEFL*, 1(1), pp. 2–14.

Turkle, S. (1997) *Life on the Screen: Identity in the Age of the Internet.* 1st Touchstone Ed ed. New York: Simon & Schuster.

Varis, P. and Wang, X. (2011) 'Superdiversity on the Internet: A Case from China', *Diversities.* 2011, 13(2). www.unesco.org/shs/diversities/vol13/issue2/, date accessed 10 July 2013.

Walker, S. (2013) 'Kiev Protesters Topple Lenin Statue', 8 December, http://www.theguardian.com, date accessed 10 December.

Wallis Simons, J. (2013) 'Children are having their Imaginations Destroyed by iPads and Video Games', *The Daily Telegraph*, Blog Page, 3 March. http://www.telegraph.co.uk, date accessed 4 March 2013.

Warschauer, M. (2004) *Technology And Social Inclusion: Rethinking The Digital Divide.* Cambridge, MA: MIT Press.

Wenger, E. (1998) *Communities of Practice: Learning, Meaning and Identity.* Cambridge: Cambridge University Press.

Werth, P. (1999) *Text Worlds: Representing Conceptual Space in Discourse*. London: Longman.

Wikipedia (2013) 'Main Page', http://en.wikipedia.org/wiki/Main_Page, date accessed 8 October 2013.

Young, S. (1996) 'Can I Come Along?' http://courses.washington.edu/hypertxt/cgi-bin/book/wordsinimages/unstablerels.html#textmon, date accessed 12 June 2013.

Zappavigna, M. (2012) *Discourse of Twitter and Social Media: How We Use Language to Create Affiliation on the Web*. London: Continuum.

Zelynskyj, S. (no date) 'The Shadow' http://courses.washington.edu/hypertxt/cgi-bin/book/wordsinimages/unstablerels.html, date accessed 12 June 2013.

Index

Aarseth, E.J., 139
adjacency pairs, 6, 26, 51, **161**
affordances, **2**, 4, 8, 9, 12, 29, 39, 60, 71, 76, 88, 98, 109, 134, 136, 145, 150–1
Allen, S., 75
Amerika, M., 95
Andrews, J., 88
　'Seattle Drift', 88–9
Azariah, D. R., 39, 45, 52
Abu Bakar, N., 25

Bakhtin, M. M., 16, 44, 58, 59, 117, 151, 153
Barr, M., 77
　'How my brain betrays me', 89–93
Barthes, R., 13, 17, 122
Barton, D., 2, 9, 17, 21, 33, 54
Barton, K., 77
　'How my brain betrays me', 89–93
Bell, Alice, 118, 139
Bell, Allen, 57, 58–9, 65, 71, 75
Bezemer, J., 23
Bhatia, V., 142–3, 159
blogs and **blogging**, 3, 8, 11, 22, 25, 33, 141, 147, 152
　j-blogs, 60, **141**, 63, 65, 68–9
　in online news, 56, **59–65**, 66–73
　in social networking sites (SNSs), 37, **39–40**, 45
　students' online blog, **25–9**
　see also Buddha Smiled; microblogging
Blommaert, J., 153, 155, 159
Bolter, J.D., 13, 17, 121
Boyd, D., 37, 39, 41, 53
Buddha Smiled, The, 8, 155–7

CDA, see Critical Discourse Analysis
Clark, U., 17

code-mixing, 141, 153–4
coherence, 30, **80**, 89, 93, 112, 115, 122, **124–6**, 130, **134–5**, **161**
cohesion, **23**, 28, **30**, 50, **80**, 83, 85, **87–9**, 110–12, 122, **124–6**, **130–5**, **137**, **161**
community
　discourse community, **7**, 39, 41, 19
　community of practice, **7**, 20
computer-mediated communication (**CMC**), **3–4**, 6–7, 12–13
conceptual patterns, **67**, **77**, **161**
Critical Discourse Analysis (CDA), 17, **57–9**, 75
Crystal, D., 6

DA, see Discourse Analysis
DeAndrea, D.C., 44, 154
Delicious, 47, **48–9**
dialogism, **44**, **151**, **161**
digital natives, **18–19**, 34
Dillon, G.L., 81, 83
Discourse Analysis (DA), 3, **12**, 17, 75
discourse world, **99–102**, 104, 108, 110, 112, 115, 127, 132, 136, **162**

Ellison, N., 37, 39, 41, 53
Ensslin, A., 128, 134, 138–9

Facebook, 3, 8, 17, **36–40**, 41, **43**, 45–6, **51**, 55, 60, 144–5, 147, **154–5**
face work, 27, **44**, **162**
Fairclough, N., 16, 75, 145–6, 159
Feng, J., 98, 118
field, 14, **23–4**, 25, 31, 51, 63, **65–6**, 81, 83, 89, 103, **108–9**, **114–15**, 122, **126–7**, **132–3**, 135, **162**
Firth, J. R., 14

Flickr, 37, 40, 54, 103, 110
folksonomy, **48**
foregrounding 88, 95, **162**, 164
Fowler, R., 68
function-advancing propositions, **100**, 104, 105, 107, 111, 114, 128, **162**
Funkhouser, C.T., 76, 94, 95

Gavins, J., 15, 99, 112, 118, 119, 131
genre, 7, 9, 29, 31, 40–3, 57, 68, 86, 122, 126, **141–5**, **152**, 159, **162**
  genre hybrids, 60, **145–8**, **149–52**, **155–7**
Gibbons, A., 118
Goffman, E., 42, 58
Grice's Maxims, **13**, 51, **162**

Halliday, M. A. K., **14**, 17, 35, 66–7, 87, 95, 100, 158, 165
Herring, S.C., 5, 31, 62, 158
heteroglossia, 59, **153**, **162**
hybridity, *see* genre hybrids
hyponymy, 23, 161, **162**

ideational meaning, **14**, 57, 77, 79, 122, 126, 132, 138, **162**, **165**
  in digital news, 65–7
identity, **2–3**, 17, 21, 36, 37, 42–3, 45, 55, 115, 126, 130, 143
  see also self-presentation
interdiscursivity, **145–6**, 148, 150–1
Internet Relayed Chat (IRC), **4–6**, 8
interpersonal meaning, **14**, 23–4, 31, 36, 79, 92, 114, **162**, **164**
  in digital news, 67–70
  and reader empowerment in hypertext fiction, 122–4
intertextuality, 59–60, 65, 127, **146**, 150–1, 155–6, **163**
IRC, *see* Internet Relayed Chat

Jackson, S., 120, 126
  Patchwork Girl, 126–30, 132, 133, 136, 139, 140, 146

Jakobson's functions of language, 15, 91, 145, **163**
j-blogs, *see* blogs
Jewitt, C., 20
Joseph, C., 102
  Flight Paths, 102–11
Joyce, M., 124, 134
  Twelve Blue, 126, 130–5, 136, 137

Kress, G. R., 14, 23, 67, 77–8

Labov's element of oral narratives, **58**, **163**
Landow, G.P., 121, 124–6, 130, 139
Lee, C., 2, 9, 17, 21, 33, 54
lexia, 84, **121–3**, 124–37, 143, 146, **163**
lexical density, 31, 46, 64, **163**
linearity, 103, **121**, 124–5, 133, 137–8, **163**
LinkedIn, 37–8, 40–1, 51, 144, 147
literacy practices, 1, 9–10, 17, **19–21**, 35, 45, **163**

Malinowski, B., 14
Martin, A., 142
Martin, J.R., 11
microblogging, **38–9**, 45, 64, 149
  see also Twitter
Miles, A., 122, 125–6, 133
modality, 28, 32, **68–9**, **102**, **163**
  in images, 79, 91–2
modal world, **15**, 101–4, 107–8, 112–13, 116, 129, 136, 138, **164**
mode, **14**, 19–21, **22–3**, 29, 80, 87, 89–90, 93, 111, 130, 136, 138, 150–2, 155, 159
multimodality, 2, 12, 17, **20**, 73, 84, 118, **164**
Murray, D., 150
  'Digital Essay', 150–2
Myers, G., 31, 35, 65, 69–70

Nelson, J., 84
  'Sydney's Siberia', 84–88

New Literacy Studies (NLS), 1, **9–10**, 12, 20, 34–5
NLS, *see* New Literacy Studies

Page, R.E., 118, 144, 147
parallelism, 91, **164**
polysemy, 89, **164**
presentational patterns, **67**, 77, **164**
Pullinger, K., 102
 Flight Paths, 102–11
Prensky, M., 18–19, 35

Rampton, B., 153, 155, 159
register, 4, 6–8, 14, 24, 26, 31, 38, 40–1, 51, 61, **68–9**, 104, 110, 114, 128, 136, 143–5, 148, 151, 158, **164**
Ryan, M.L., 132

Schneider, R., 125
self-presentation, 36, 39, 42–5, 48, 156, 158
 see also identity
SFL, *see* Systemic Functional Linguistics
Short, M., 95, 119
Snyder, I., 35
SNS, *see* social networking site
Social media, *see* social networking site
social networking site (SNS), 11, **36–55**, 60–1, 64, 94, 103, 143–5, 147–9, 154
 digital talk in SNSs, 51–3
 digital text in SNSs, 46–51
 discourse communities in SNSs, 40–2
 self-presentation in SNSs, 42–5
Stephens, P., 120
 'Samantha in Winter', 135–7
Stockwell, P., 102
superdiversity, 141, **153–6**, 159–60, **164**
Swales, J.M., 7, 40, 142

synonymy, 23, 30, 50, 110, 112, 134, **161**, **164**
Systemic Functional Linguistics (SFL), **14–15**, 17, 23, 35, 46, 54, 57, 65, 80, 95, 99–100, 111, 122, 142
 see also field; Halliday; ideational meaning; interpersonal meaning; mode; tenor; textual meaning; transitivity

Tagg, C., 55
tenor, 14, 24, 26, 27, 31–2, 38, 43, 51, 79, 81, 83, 89, 91, 95, 104, 109–10, 112–14, 128, 136, 138, 158, **162**, **164**
textual meaning, **14**, 18, 21–3, 28–30, 42, 80, 89, 110, 112, 122, 134, **164**
 in digital news, 71–3
 in hypertext fiction, 124–6
text world, **100–2**, 103–5, 107–16, 127, 129, 132–4, 135–6, **165**
Text World Theory (TWT), **99–102**, 118–9
 see also discourse world; function-advancing propositions; modal world; text world; world-building elements
Thurlow, C., 3
transitivity, 57, 67, 77–8, 100, **165**
Tremayne, M., 63, 71
Trimarco, P., 25
Tumblr, 39–40, 45, 55, 64
Turkle, S., 3
Twitter, 8, 17, **37–40**, 45, 47, 49, **52–3**, 55, 60, 63–4, 98, 118, 145–7
TWT, *see* Text World Theory

van Leeuwen, T., 14, 67, 77–8
virtual learning environment (VLE), 9, **22**, 25, 30, 152
VLE, *see* virtual learning environment

Wenger, E., 7
Werth, P., 15–16, 101, 119
Wikipedia, 9, 10, **29–33**, 35, 37, 49, 125, 144, 148
world-building elements, **100–1**, 104, 105, 107, 113, 119, 127–8, 131–2, **165**

YouTube, 37, 43, 46, 49, 60, 89, 145, 148, 154

Zappavigna, M., 41, 52, 55
Zelynskyj, S., 81
'The Shadow', 81–3